# *the* BUSINESS *of* DESIGN

# the BUSINESS of DESIGN

*of*

Joseph DeSetto

DELMAR
CENGAGE Learning  Australia Canada Mexico Singapore Spain United Kingdom United States

**The Business of Design**
**Joseph DeSetto**

Vice President, Career and Professional
Editorial: Dave Garza

Director of Learning Solutions:
Sandy Clark

Acquisitions Editor: James Gish

Managing Editor: Larry Main

Product Manager: Nicole Calisi

Editorial Assistant: Sarah Timm

Vice President, Career and Professional
Marketing: Jennifer McAvey

Marketing Director: Debbie Yarnell

Marketing Manager: Erin Brennan

Marketing Coordinator:
Jonathan Sheehan

Production Director: Wendy Troeger

Production Manager: Stacy Masucci

Senior Content Project Manager:
Kathryn B. Kucharek

Art Director: Joy Kocsis

Technology Project Manager:
Christopher Catalina

Production Technology Analyst:
Thomas Stover

For product information and technology assistance, contact us at
**Professional & Career Group Customer Support, 1-800-648-7450**

For permission to use material from this text or product,
submit all requests online at **cengage.com/permissions.**
Further permissions questions can be e-mailed to
**permissionrequest@cengage.com.**

Library of Congress Control Number: 2008926707

ISBN 13: 978-1-4283-2229-5
ISBN 10: 1-4283-2229-9

**Delmar Cengage Learning**
5 Maxwell Drive
Clifton Park, NY 12065-2919
USA

Cengage Learning products are represented in Canada by Nelson Education, Ltd.

For your lifelong learning solutions, visit **delmar.cengage.com**
Visit our corporate web site at **cengage.com.**

### NOTICE TO THE READER

Printed in Canada
1 2 3 4 5 6 7 12 11 10 09 08

# *contents*

# *preface*

## INTENDED AUDIENCE

*The Business of Design* is the definitive book to teach business to artists pursuing a career in design. For many years, university design curriculums and books have been able to successfully teach the thought, process, and method of creating high impact corporate communications, yet many students still begin their career—and even advance into senior positions or start their own design firms—with only a limited understanding of the business and industry that employs these talents. This text was created to fill that void and better prepare designers to choose employers, work with clients, and successfully navigate a creative career.

## BACKGROUND

In this text, we focus mainly on visual design, though many other areas of practice—interiors, interactive, industrial—follow similar conventions and share the same challenges. This text is written for anyone in the design field to use, and though primarily intended for university classroom use, it is written in a more approachable, conversational style than the usual formal approach of a business textbook. Charts and graphs are kept to a minimum and engaging illustrations are used wherever possible to aid the visual learner. The book is also full of world-class design work from many of North America's top firms to inspire students and add context to the business content presented here.

This book is not intended to replace an MBA or instill all the knowledge business owners and executives acquire first hand in the course of running a design business. In the following pages we want you to understand enough about business that you see where your work fits, why it has value, and how to shape your career.

This book was created from a list I kept over 7 years of teaching interactive design and development to university design students. As a business school graduate teaching artists, the most frequent hallway questions from students were always about proposals, billable rates, contracts, and legal issues. Rather than answer these on my own in this text, I also interviewed some of the most accomplished and award-winning principals, art directors, and designers in North America to supplement my own experience as a freelancer and owner of a small firm. Their words are quoted here directly in a few cases, but these interviews were also critical to developing the final list of topics and areas of emphasis.

# TEXTBOOK ORGANIZATION

This book first introduces the creative industry. Chapter 1 looks at recent salary information for both entry level and more accomplished designers. In this chapter we'll also look at the major employer types and compare the jobs of in-house art departments to design firms.

Chapter 2 explores the way business thinking differs from creative or artistic pursuits. Although it is, of course, stereotyping to a certain degree to explain how any group sees the world, there are significant differences to learn between the method of the artist and the calculation of the businessperson. Understanding these differences can help a designer communicate in terms coworkers, clients, and supervisors trained in business will understand and appreciate.

Next, we explore the jobs in the industry. The variety of areas that require design training is as expansive as business itself, but we'll narrow our focus to the most common job titles to get a sense of how designers move from production to management in the course of a career.

Marketing, the next major topic we cover in depth is not a how-to, as designers by nature will use their own creativity for specific campaigns. Instead, we look at how business relies on marketing for differentiation. This differentiation applies to job applicants, suppliers, and products, so understanding how to formulate a unique position in the market is the focus here. The system used in some form by most organizations, the funnel, introduces the designer to the sales process of turning leads into buyers.

In Proposals and Projects, we'll look at calculating the elusive hourly billable rate, including a lengthy comparison of salary to freelance income. There are a few common ways to bill clients, and these options are also presented in this chapter. Finally, we cover the basics of project management and learn the importance of documenting decisions in today's business environment.

There is no free legal advice in the following chapter, but we will review the major types of intellectual property—copyright, trademarks, and patents. Because almost everything you'll create as a professional designer is intellectual property in some form, the laws surrounding the profession are critical to learn before you sign away rights to your work or land on the wrong end of a legal dispute. Along with intellectual property, there are contractual issues to employment that you should understand, as well.

Much of your work will be collaborative, and many of the images, typefaces, and illustrations that you'll use will be licensed for that use. In Design Assets, we look at the common licensing and pricing models and see how these products can be legally used for your projects.

To conclude this book, we begin to learn what it takes to start your own firm. There are many decisions that must be made to ensure a successful business, and the first of them will probably be the type of legal structure your firm will have. We look at the differences in liability, and even a few tax items, between going on your own as corporation and partnership.

# FEATURES

## About the DVD

In a fast-paced nineteen days in the spring of 2008, I visited four cities to conduct interviews for the DVD included in the back of this text. New York and San Francisco were the obvious places to start, as acclaimed work from these design capitals still draws many talented designers to either start their career or establish their own firms within walking distance of Fortune 500 accounts.

In New York, David Schimmel of And Partners, David Lipkin of Method, Marko Bon, the Global Creative Architect for an internationally known fashion label and two of his staff designers, and Connecticut-based Alexander Isley all offered their insight on camera. Their experiences, influences, and current firms are all very different, and each has a unique perspective to offer students of design.

In San Francisco, the Senior Vice President of Brand Integration for Publicis & Hal Riney, Ken Cook, offered an hour of his thoughts. Kenn Fine and his crew at Fine Design Group were gracious hosts and offered great insight, at least once I finally found their office. Earlier that morning, Erik Adams and Sharrie Brooks offered their perspectives from the beautiful space of Cahan and Associates.

Away from the busy streets of New York and San Francisco, thousands of smaller firms are thriving. I chose only two for the DVD, but both were great hosts with several people willing to interview. A two-story building in Reno, Nevada, is the busy office of The Glenn Group. Going through a recent merger with another Reno agency, the firm still found the time to interview, including Paul Hamill, Amy Lockhart, Brian Johnson, and Oz Mendoza. Paul, their associate creative director, traded life in the crowded Bay Area for a commute over a snowy mountain pass to live near the outdoors.

I started the interviews with a trip to Charlotte, North Carolina. In a brand new office park in the booming south Charlotte suburbs is Addison Whitney. The agency does work for major brands in several industries, including medical, technology, and food. Kim Davis, the Director of Visual Branding, and her staff hosted me for two days, including a lunchtime trip for some authentic southern barbeque.

The DVD allowed me to present these talented individuals directly, and while the content is not an exact match of any one chapter, the focus of each interview is on the business, the industry, and what designers need to know starting out. My goal was to make the DVD as relevant to each student as it would be to have a few minutes alone with each of these extremely busy people, and I hope you enjoy and learn from them as they recount their experiences. I want to sincerely thank each of the interviewees for their time and for their role in *The Business of Design*.

# ACKNOWLEDGMENTS

I first want to thank my parents for encouraging me to never stop learning, for the sacrifices they made so I would have the opportunity to succeed, and for giving me the freedom to find my own path through life.

I also want to thank Dan and Maria, who have no idea how much I learned from them. My brother and sister are the real artists in the family, and introduced me to drawing, decent music, story structure, The Force, and other skills I still use to make a living in the creative field. I hope they both quit their responsible day jobs one day and do something like this instead.

Thanks Tom. You also encouraged my creativity every chance you had and taught me my forehand, as well as weird stuff like binary math and 3D chess. A great teacher is never really gone, as every student that learns something from me has you to thank, as well.

I want to thank Amanda, the love of my life. She lives in a partially restored house with me because I allocate an inordinate amount of time to projects that I find creatively stimulating, like writing, and to my other grandiose ideas. I love you, look forward to our life together, and appreciate your patience with my artistic side.

Thanks to Matt McEachern, a very talented illustrator and designer who knew very little about business. Our work together was the first time I realized these topics should be taught to artists, or that my business school education was radically different from what creative people learn in school. Thanks to Trish for the introduction, circa 1999.

Thanks to James Bennett, my former boss and the author of several Cengage Learning titles, including *Design Fundamentals for New Media.* James is as good a friend and advisor as you'll ever find in the political world of a modern university, and unselfishly encouraged his publisher to consider me as an author.

Thanks to Brent Britton, the intellectual property guru that was gracious enough to teach me everything I needed to know about legal issues for designers over beverages and fish tacos at The Fly, complete with PowerPoint slides. It is a rare individual that is both as successful as Brent and as willing to invest their time to help others succeed. One reviewer of an early draft of this book called the legal chapter "the best explanation of these topics I've seen" and I have Brent to thank for that.

Thanks to Chris Collins for perspective when I thought this project would never end and for teaching me how a true artist sees the world without the constraint of corporate clients, deadlines, or other pressures students of this text will face in their careers.

Thanks to Jim Gish and Nicole Calisi at Cengage Learning. Jim got into this project from the start and made it happen. The good fortune of an experienced Acquisitions Editor that believed in my project was the reason I had the opportunity to write for the past year. Nicole has helped me navigate the often frustrating details of writing a book for a major publisher, and without her involvement this would undoubtedly still be a pile of Word documents on my Mac or a 400-page blog on TypePad and not a real, complete book in your hands.

I also want to thank sincerely the rest of the team at Cengage for their role in the completion of this book. Because of the arrangement of deadlines, I unfortunately cannot say who exactly, beyond Jim and Nicole, contributed in what way, but please remember as you read this that a talented team of people is required to put this together. The author is simply the lead singer for the project and everyone else on the tour bus brings his or her own skills and experience to this tune. Without them, all these words are just singing in the shower instead of rocking out at campuses around the country.

For their time and consideration in interviewing for *The Business of Design*, I want to thank the following creative people. You contributed to the education of all those that read this book, as well as my own.

| | | |
|---|---|---|
| Mark Abernethy | Kristin Everidge | Robert Lee |
| Erik Adams | Paul Evers | David Lipkin |
| Noelle Bates | Kenn Fine | Amy Lockhart |
| Marko Bon | John Fisher | Sam Maclay |
| Sunny Bonnell | Doug Grimmett | Rob Marsh |
| Sharrie Brooks | Paul Hamill | Mark McDevitt |
| Stan Byers | Sarah Hans | Tim McGrath |
| Melissa Chan | Bret Hummel | Oswaldo Mendoza |
| Yong Cho | Nick Irwin | Audelino Moreno |
| Paul Curtin | Alex Isley | Jon Pritzl |
| Harris Damashek | Brian Johnson | Clint! Runge |
| Kim Davis | Josh Kelly | Rita Sasges |
| Matt Diefenbach | Benjamin Kinzer | David Schimmel |
| Kieron Dwyer | David Lai | Melissa Wygant |

# THE CREATIVE INDUSTRY

1

# introduction

Design reaches every industry around the world in some form. At its core, design is a method of solving problems. A designer must learn how their work is one piece of a much larger business puzzle. In this chapter, we introduce the industry, including a look at the amount of revenue design generates and what designers can expect to earn.

# objectives

**Understanding the size and revenue of an average design firm.**

**The creative services industry by total revenue and number of firms in operation.**

**Average salaries in the profession.**

# THE BUSINESS OF DESIGN

Artists have not traditionally enjoyed the cold impersonal logic of the mechanisms of business. Business leaders have similarly never shown much reverence for or understanding of the creative process. When the two seemingly opposite worlds collide, the results have been extraordinary and often change entire industries. As such, many of the largest and most respected brands in the world understand both the emotional connections with customers that only art can create and have a firm grasp of the financial and legal realities that allow the business to continue to operate successfully. Customers generally do not think of an advanced global distribution system when they send a FedEx, tons of fuel and expert logistics when they fly Southwest Airlines, or of electrons buzzing around a circuit board inside their Mac—they only know the brand. This is the intersection of art and commerce, and much like the best brand managers and marketers understand enough about design process to get the most out of it, the most effective and sought after designers understand business.

As a design career progresses, business starts to play a more and more important role. The first, and most direct, is that many accomplished designers want to start their own firms and—despite the fantasy of pure creative freedom—realize quickly that a firm is a small business and not immune from taxes, employment issues, office space, lawsuits, and every other distraction. A designer that stays with a firm will still find their role move from color and layout to strategic planning, target demographics, and cost issues. Finally, a designer that works for a creative department of a larger company will move up the ladder and, in a management role, still confront business issues such as departmental budgets.

# THE INDUSTRY

An interesting dynamic of creative services as a business is that there is no single dominant brand. Unlike many other industries that see a small number of companies grow into global titans, the design business is fragmented. There are a few firms that have offices around the world, and many expand their services well beyond design into advertising brokerage and brand management. These multidisciplinary firms that handle a few of the largest accounts aside, design—the business of creating brands—does not have a small group of leading brands. There are no household names in design, as many designers find when they start to sort through the industry trying to find the Microsoft, Nike, and Wal-Mart of creative services. Even the larger firms with services spanning advertising, architecture, and industrial design—BBDO, Pentagram, IDEO, for example—are not as recognized as their clients—Pepsi, Citibank, Xerox, respectively. Hoovers (a division of Dun and Bradstreet, a leading provider of business information and statistics) estimates that the fifty largest firms in the world account for less than 20% of the revenue in the graphic design industry. This is in stark contrast to other large industries that are dominated by a few large companies (see Figure 1–1). The automobile manufacturing industry generates $250 billion a year, but only eight companies account for more than 90% of the revenue. The music industry earns $15 billion annually—almost twice as much as graphic design—but only eight companies earn 80% of this amount.

With firms that employ hundreds of people taking such a relatively small amount of the available design work, small firms and freelancers make up the vast majority of professional creative

## CONSOLIDATED INDUSTRIES VS. GRAPHIC DESIGN

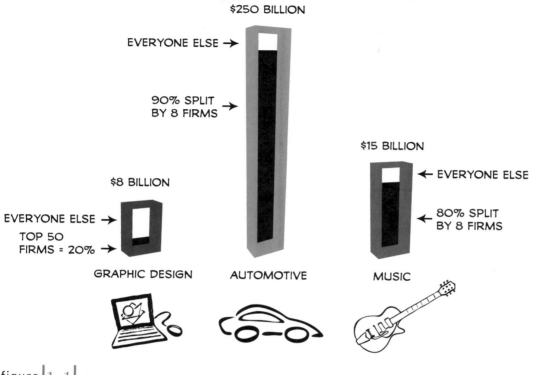

figure |1–1|

Traditional industries such as automotive and music bring in more total revenue than graphic design, but most of the money is split by very few companies—dominant brands like Toyota or Universal. In design, the top fifty firms only account for 20% of the revenue generated by the industry.

services businesses. It is estimated that 30% of the revenue in graphic design goes to self-employed designers. An average graphic design firm, according to Hoovers, has only one location, less than four people, and brings in around $500,000. Although this much revenue might sound like enough to pay off a school loan or two, it puts most design firms in the category of a very small business. Many of the firms interviewed for this book, for example, were six- to ten-person operations and several firm principals noted that growing too large or too fast was not desirable or necessary for continued success in a creative business.

Nationally, there are more than 16,000 companies classified as graphic design firms and the total revenue is estimated around $8 billion. Although that creates the nice round average of $500,000 per firm, the reality of the business is that competitive pressures, rising small business costs (office space, health insurance, etc.), and competition from new business models mean that the industry is segmenting into "haves"—thriving firms with stellar reputations that can command premium rates and are able to decline work—and "have-nots"—firms that will have to fold.

The expense of running a firm also creates the situation in some specialties that freelancers are making more than the people hiring them. One principal who runs a highly acclaimed niche firm explained, "If I was getting out of school today and did [the design specialty] I would freelance instead."

There is still tremendous opportunity in design as media savvy, image-conscious companies, which have an endless supply of messages to communicate, increasingly drive the economy. The demand for professional design creates supply, and there are thousands of graduates each year in graphic design, web design, and other related disciplines competing to fill the job openings at design firms. Starting salaries in design are usually not very high, but designers with talent, work ethic, and—perhaps as important—the ability to communicate their work to clients will move up the pay scale quickly and have more work than they can handle.

Almost every designer interviewed for this book indicated that demands from clients have never been higher. Great design is everywhere and clients are surrounded by work that may not even have been possible years ago. Increasingly advanced graphics software has now enabled visual designers—from freelancers to corporate art departments—to create literally anything imaginable. With the bar this high and the demands to deliver work faster and under budget, design can be a stressful profession and not for everyone, or even every artist.

# COMPENSATION

With all the pressure to create on tight deadlines, the natural question for aspiring designers is whether the job is worth it. Every successful designer we spoke to had a version of the same belief—design is something you have to love to do when you get out of school, and you have to stay focused on doing great work. If you do great work, your peers and clients will notice. When that happens, you will make a better than average living doing what you love to do.

 Although it is true many designers worked on low paying jobs to fine-tune their skills before moving up and eventually managing huge projects for notable clients, there is still a need to look at the numbers to see where you may start your career and where you could go from there.

According the U.S. Bureau of Labor Statistics, there were just over 190,000 individuals working in the country as a graphic designer in May 2006. The mean hourly wage was $21.07. The mean annual wage was $43,830 (see Figure 1–2). The top 10% earned over $53,000 a year or $33 an hour. The lowest earning 10% of graphic designers made just over $10 an hour and $24,000 a year.

The government has a separate classification for art directors, though their definition sounds much like the job description of many graphic designers: *Formulate design concepts and presentation approaches, and direct workers engaged in art work, layout design, and copy writing for visual communications media, such as magazines, books, newspapers, and packaging.*

Of the just over 31,000 people identified as art directors, the mean hourly wage in 2006 was $37.70 (see Figure 1–3). The mean annual wage was $78,420. The top 10% reached an income of over $130,000 a year or $64.95 an hour. The lowest paid 10% of art directors made around $38,000 or $18 an hour. Interestingly, higher incomes in major design cities like New York and Los Angeles were much more pronounced among art directors than graphic designers.

## MEAN EARNINGS, US BUREAU OF LABOR STATISTICS, GRAPHIC DESIGNERS

figure 1–2

According to the U.S. Bureau of Labor Statistics, designers earned between $24,000 and $53,000 a year in 2006, with a median salary of $43,830.

$24,000
LOWEST 10%  ←—— $43,830 ——→  $53,000
TOP 10%

ANNUAL SALARY, 2006

$10  ←—— $21.07 ——→  $33

HOURLY WAGE, 2006

## MEAN EARNINGS, US BUREAU OF LABOR STATISTICS, ART DIRECTOR

figure 1–3

According to the U.S. Bureau of Labor Statistics, Art Directors earned between $38,000 and over $130,000 a year in 2006, with a median salary of $78,420.

$38,000
LOWEST 10%  ←—— $78,420 ——→  $130,000
HIGHEST 10%

ANNUAL SALARY

$18  ←—— 0 ——→  $64.95

HOURLY WAGE

In 2004, there were 228,000 employed graphic designers. The government statistics lists only 30% of designers as freelancers, but note that "many" full-time designers also freelance. This trait is common to the profession but fairly unique among other jobs—your dentist probably does not leave the office and fix teeth from home. Freelancing is also a difficult practice to track with statistics, as taking design work outside a firm could be something a designer does once a year as a favor to a friend or a full-time pursuit as one builds toward starting their own practice. LogoWorks, for example, an online identity creation company, indicated that many of their freelance designers are employed full time with other creative firms and more than half had over 5 years of experience. The motivations for taking work outside of the firm vary, and some experienced designers use quick freelance projects to keep their skills sharp after a long day of meetings and management paperwork.

AIGA, the professional association for design, and Aquent, a global staffing company, partner to conduct a thorough survey of design professionals each year. The result is more comprehensive than the government statistics and delves into details such as the amount of designers with medical insurance (95% for designers in firms of ten people or larger) and company vehicles (about 5 to 7%, depending on the size of the firm). In 2007, the AIGA/Aquent survey showed "solo designers"—freelancers and single person design firms—with a median annual income of $60,000. Art Directors reported a median income of $70,000—lower than the government stats— but Creative Directors (also called Design Directors at some firms) landed on a median income of $90,000, with the top 25% at $116,000 a year. The category most students find themselves in, entry-level designers, earned a median income of $35,000 a year with only a $5,000 difference in either direction for the highest and lowest earners.

Finally, the owners of design firms, often carrying the title of Principal, President, or Partner, do tend to earn over $100,000 a year as the business becomes successful. This is not the entire picture, however, because a well-managed firm is an asset that can be sold or merged with another company for a significant amount. To build a firm to this level, the business must have strong relationships with stable clients and an accurate accounting of the property, both tangible and intangible, owned by the firm.

All of these income statistics use medians instead of averages to give a more realistic picture of what each role earns. An average adds all the survey participants' income and divides by the total number of people. The problem with using averages in this situation is an unreasonably low amount—the nephew of the boss getting some experience for minimum wage before leaving for art school—or a wildly high amount—the well-connected designer who takes only high paying work from personal friends in Hollywood and Wall Street—would skew the number. Using a median, statisticians use the extreme cases to effectively cancel each other out. For every high salary, there is a low salary until the middle of the group is found.

Compare the average of ten designers making the following amounts for their annual income with the median of the same group:

- $1,200,000
- $120,000
- $75,000
- $56,000
- $50,000
- $48,000
- $40,000
- $38,000

- $32,000
- $18,000

The median for this group is $49,000, or half way between the fifth and sixth earner out of ten. The average salary is $167,700 (see Figure 1–5). Clearly if you were going to take a job where these salaries were offered, you would have a much more accurate idea of your potential salary from the median than from the average. Another way to look at a median is that half of the people in the group earn more than that person and half earn less. In design, as in many professions, where you fall within that group will depend on many factors.

---

**Q&A Ask the Pros:**
**Learning Beyond Design**
**Doug Grimmett, Primal Screen**

*Q: What advice would you give students pursuing a career in design?*
A: You are not wasting your time learning other things. I hear students talk about "Why do I have to learn physics or calculus or history?" It is very important, because that is what we do. We interpret the culture. We have to know a little about a lot of things. Every project is a new learning opportunity. You can master Photoshop or After Effects, but what are you going to do with it? What do you have to say? What is your vision?

---

# THE EMPLOYERS

You have put in the hours to learn your craft, and you have several types of firms you can now target as employers. Although virtually any business is a potential lead, we want to be a bit more specific in our pursuit of a name to grace your first (real) business card. Potential employers are usually categorized as small design firm, large design firm, or in-house design staff. Each has its advantages and disadvantages, so take the time to meet with anyone that wants to offer a position because you may end up going in a direction you would not have thought would appeal to you.

---

There is no perfect first job. You have to start somewhere though, and businesses around the world need skills just like yours. Do not turn your back on your talent and the time you have spent to get this far if you do not land something immediately. You will rarely be more attractive to employers than you are as a recent graduate. The salary you require is relatively low. Your skills are in all likelihood either on the leading edge or at least current. You probably do not have the jaded, cynical perspective of so many of the field's veterans, and if you do it is because of what you have read or heard about, not experienced firsthand. There is an unfortunately high amount of very talented people in the arts who for one reason or another, do not take that first step to make a career of it. There are plenty of business owners, executives, and creative directors who are looking for you. It may take a few months, but find a way into the field.

# In-House

In-house design includes all the creative work produced within art, marketing, advertising, and creative departments for the use of the employer firm (see Figure 1–4). The business itself is your employer and primary client. This can be a relatively small firm that has a two-person art department or a major global brand that has a whole floor full of people working on various campaigns and products. Either way, in-house work means the client is your coworker. Instead of having clients in many different industries and working on a specific project, in-house designers work on the core products and service of their own employer.

In-house has its perks, and they are the perks of working for a large company in general. Usually the benefits package is valuable, and it will always help to have a name on your resume that your next potential employer will immediately know. As such, in-house work is not a bad place to start for a designer, but can also be an attractive option later in your career, as well. As an in-house designer, you will usually have a little more job security than at a consultancy and much more than a starting freelancer. In-house work will also give you the opportunity to work with the same team for a period of time and see how an entire yearlong business cycle looks from the inside, from the annual report to the seasonal promotions. This can be great experience when you do decide to go on your own or work for a consultancy. The downside of in-house is that you are working within the best practices of a single client, your employer, not of many clients in a variety of industries. You will maintain the standards put forth by your employer's identity system, which will provide you a structure, but can become tedious to use over a number of years.

## IN-HOUSE WORK

USUALLY LARGE,
RELATIVELY STABLE

BENEFITS (INSURANCE, STOCK, ETC.)

LEARN COMPLETE LIFESTYLE
AND SEASONAL USE OF BRAND

LEARN DESIGN FROM CORPORATE
PERSPECTIVE

RESUME PADDING

SAME BRAND FOR MONTHS OR
YEARS = TEDIOUS/BORING

LIMITED EXPERIENCE IN OTHER
INDUSTRIES

DESIGN JUST ANOTHER DEPT.
IN LARGER PICTURE

figure |1–4|

In-house work is usually not as diverse as a traditional design agency might offer, but can provide good exposure to how brands are managed along with the usual perks of a larger company such as retirement plans and relatively stable employment.

# Small Firm

Not everyone wants to work in the art department of a large organization, and many design graduates get their start working for small design studios. These firms are primarily consulting businesses; instead of solely generating recommendations for clients they also produce the work—ads, identities, and even new products. Although many advertising firms are owned by large global businesses, small shops dominate the design landscape. In a small design firm, clients from a variety of industries with diverse requirements keep work fast paced and interesting (see Figure 1–5).

Many smaller shops specialize in the niche areas of design, from interactive online games to architectural graphics. A small firm has to keep designers busy to keep the cash flow going and the doors open though, so work outside of specialty can come in at any time if a preferred client needs something done. In a small shop, a new designer is likely to get plenty of hands-on experience and more creative freedom, at least on the more experimental clients, than they would see from a more established practice. Designers in a small firm will often act as mentors to new designers, as the demands of project require everyone get up to speed quickly.

Of course, all this excitement is not for everyone. Small firms in every industry have the same issues, and may not be able to afford health benefits, paid vacation, or always have the latest software to use. The firm may only be known locally or regionally, as well, so when it is time to move on you will be job hunting without the big name experience. Plenty of art directors and other design principals know that a resume full of big name clients might mean more talent,

## SMALL DESIGN FIRM

FAST PACED

CLIENTS ACROSS MANY
INDUSTRIES

HIGHLY COLLABORATIVE

DESIGN IS CORE FOCUS, NOT JUST
DEPT. OF BIG ENTITY

SMALL BUSINESS: OFTEN
OFFER LESS BENEFITS

LIMITED TIME TO FOCUS OUTSIDE
IMMEDIATE CLIENT REQUESTS

LIMITED ROOM FOR PROMOTION

figure |1–5|

Small design firms are the norm in the industry, and often provide a fast-paced environment of collaboration with clients in many industries. A small design firm may not provide the same benefits as an in-house employer, and deadline-oriented, varied assignments mean skills in niche design areas have limited time to develop.

but high-profile work can help you get past the first glance of human resources and recruiting agencies. Finally, the breadth of experience may come at the expense of depth, as you may get to work with a client only once and not do the same assignment enough to improve your skills compared to an in-house designer who might have so much of the same work that it becomes routine.

# Large Firm

Some of these small, seemingly manic design firms we just described grow into large consultancies with international clients and multiple offices. These firms are often found in advertising, where brands must plan large-scale campaigns across entire regions with many types of media tied to the equation. Some of these relationships between large companies and their advertising consultants are long established, and it would not be feasible or cost-effective for a McDonalds or Nike to use hundreds of small, niche firms to handle their accounts. Your opportunity as a designer varies with the firm, but will likely fall toward maintaining and updating existing accounts and production-level work. These large firms do offer the opportunity to learn the design business from the perspective of some of its largest customers (see Figure 1–6). Another advantage of a larger firm is that you may get involved with higher profile, more widely circulated work than you would at a smaller shop.

Working for a large firm means you will likely start on lesser accounts and less interesting assignments. Large firms may not give a new designer much creative freedom, and will have much more process in place for handling each type of work. Projects will also tend to be longer, as the corporate approval and review process is far more involved than the speed of smaller clients that need work produced quickly.

## LARGE FIRM/AGENCY

| + | − |
|---|---|
| BIG NAME CLIENTS | LIMITED CREATIVE FREEDOM |
| LEARN INDUSTRY FROM LARGEST CUSTOMERS | HEIRARCHY TO FOLLOW |
| | LONG APPROVAL CYCLE AND MULTIYEAR PROJECT PLANNING |

figure |1–6|

A large firm enables you to learn from clients that may include the world's most known brands, but your personal creative freedom on such accounts will be limited until you work your way into a more senior role.

# Freelance

Another option, without the full leap into entrepreneurship we discuss later—see Chapter 8—is freelance work. You may not be able to find an entry-level job right away that suits your needs when you consider skills, creative freedom, benefits, location, commute, and other factors. You have no reason to idly watch the days pass though, as many design jobs are sent to freelance workers. Freelance tends to be a feast or famine scenario when you first start out, but if you learn how to market yourself and set your rates appropriately—all topics we cover in this text—you should be able to get assignments to either bridge the employment gap from college to professional or make a full-time living as a freelance pro. Technology has made some of the most challenging hurdles of freelance work, such as proximity to major design cities, less relevant than it once was and if you have the skills, going on your own might be a suitable option (see Figure 1–7).

Freelance work is a business of one though, and you must balance a lot of variables to do it right. Your client's needs and your own standard of living must match up. Too much work, or on too tight a schedule, can be just as difficult to deal with as having to work a second job to survive. You have to be able to find and secure work, which means many areas an employer would handle for you are now on your to-do list.

The benefit of freelance work starts to sink in when you commute across the living room floor in your slippers and turn your computer on for your shift. No, all freelance work is not home-based, but many clients are concerned primarily with the end product and do not micromanage the work

## FREELANCE

| **+** | **–** |
|---|---|
| YOU ARE YOUR OWN BUSINESS | NO CLIENTS = NO MONEY |
| SET YOUR RATES APPROPRIATELY | OFTEN HARD TO BALANCE DOING WORK AND LOOKING FOR NEW CLIENTS |
| GOOD EXPERIENCE SELLING WORK | SMALL BUSINESS TAX/LIABILITY ISSUES |
| CAN LEAD TO FULL-TIME POSITION | |
| OFTEN WORK AT HOME OR REMOTELY | |

figure |1–7|

Freelance work allows you to choose your clients and projects, set your own rates, and often work off-site, but can be a difficult cycle of being extremely busy to looking for work until a good base of clients is developed.

they send out. Freelance work can also be on-site with a client or in-house team that needs to supplement their staff for an assignment. In this case, you bill your time, usually hourly, but work alongside salary employees. In either case, freelance assignments can be a great way to introduce your skills to employers. For many design employers, their ability to add staff depends on budgets and the demands of business change quickly. If you are able to get on the shortlist of designers to handle freelance work, you may be called for an interview as soon as the employer can fit your salary into their plans.

| **THE BOTTOM LINE** | • Unlike many other industries that see a small number of companies dominate the industry, the graphic design business is fragmented into many small firms and independent designers. |
| --- | --- |
| | • The fifty largest graphic design firms in the world account for less than 20% of the $8 billion in revenue generated in the industry. |
| | • The in-house design includes all the creative work produced within art, marketing, advertising, and creative departments for the use of the employer firm. |
| | • In a small design firm, clients from a variety of industries with diverse requirements keep work fast paced and interesting. |
| | • Large firms offer the opportunity to learn the design business from the perspective of some of its largest customers and may involve you in higher profile, more widely circulated work than a smaller shop. |

# 2

HOW BUSINESS THINKS

# introduction

The education of a designer, both formally and informally, is quite different from many of the other professions in the business world. Business thinking is based on reducing risk, working with known facts, and using numbers to support conclusions. In this chapter, we look at how understanding these differences can improve a designer's ability to communicate and advance in the field.

# objectives

**How business places a heavy emphasis on logic and numbers.**

**The profit motive and how it drives decision making.**

**The emphasis in business for predictable results that can be duplicated.**

**Why pressure to make a profit pushes managers to stay with the status quo.**

**The key distinction between running a business and having a job.**

**The competitive advantage of quality.**

**How innovation has become a more important advantage to business.**

# THE BUSINESS WORLDVIEW

The first thing aspiring professional designers need to understand about business is that few of the people you will work with in your career—clients, suppliers, managers—will share your skills, training, or way of approaching problems. Many of your coworkers do not see the world through the lens of an artist. This creates an array of misunderstandings. Many designers feel that business managers do not "get it"—good design and how it comes to fruition. Many business managers, conversely, know they need the design group but are unfamiliar with the creative process. From both the conservative approach of forcing internal design processes into existing ways of doing business to the fanciful view that bringing artists into the conversation will turn a bad product good, business executives still do not see the whole picture of design. So creates the invisible wall of business and design—the wall between profit motive and artistic sensibilities. It starts very early in an artist's career—in school. While your future coworkers in business programs around the world are being taught to analyze data or plot trends, you are trained to create something that is off those same charts in a radical new direction. Designers are trained to create the next big thing from inspiration that spans the breadth and depth of their experience. Many business students are taught to manage the last big thing, keep a watchful eye for flaws and defects, and pay close attention to the gyrations of the current, known, identifiable competition. Is it any wonder that design—while certainly important to business—is widely misunderstood, mismanaged, and applied to business problems in a rather distant, hope-for-the-best manner? (see Figure 2–1).

figure | 2–1 |

## TWO WORLDS, ONE WORKFORCE

A quick comparison between courses taught in a typical business curriculum and courses in a design program helps explain the different worldviews of professionals with these degrees.

| BUSINESS SCHOOL | DESIGN SCHOOL |
|---|---|
| QUANTITATIVE METHODS | PAGE LAYOUT |
| MICROECONOMICS | TYPOGRAPHY |
| INFO. SYSTEMS DESIGN | ILLUSTRATION |
| OPERATIONS MANAGEMENT | DIGITAL IMAGES |
| STATISTICS | DRAWING |
| APPLIED CALCULUS | 3-D MODELLING |

## Case Study: Lessons from the Pros: Addison Whitney

Brands are often developed or polished to make them more appealing to a buyer. In the process of being divested by owner, BP®, Amoco Fabrics and Fibers Company (AFFC) approached Addison Whitney® to develop its new corporate identity. The project deliverables included logo, stationery system, and standards manual. Headquartered in Austell, GA, AFFC is a leading producer of synthetic fabrics throughout the world. After AFFC selected Propex® Fabrics as its new corporate name, Addison Whitney developed the corresponding visual identity and collateral. The Propex Fabrics logo features an abstract representation of woven fabric integrated in the letter "O" to illustrate a connection to the fabrics industry. A bold red and black color palette was selected to communicate strength and quality products, as well as stand out from competitors (see Figure 2–2).

figure | 2–2 |

Client: BP Amoco Fabrics Co.

Project: Propex Fabrics Corporate Identity

Creative Team: Kimberlee Davis (Creative Lead), Trey Walsh, and Kristin Everidg

The good news—though it may take a while to reach any given employer—is that business is trying to understand design and going to great lengths to train their management in the ways, habits, and workflow of the artist. From heralded new master's degree programs at leading universities to the quiet, but increasingly frequent mention of design in stalwart business publications such as *Fortune* magazine and the *Wall Street Journal,* artists—and how you do what you do—are in demand not only for skills, but also for their worldview and approach to problems.

Such cultural change toward acceptance of artists, however positive it may sound, is slow in the business world. Much like advertising evolved from necessary evil—how do you keep sales of carbonated, sugary water from slipping in the winter months?—to being the backbone of global corporate communication, design is gradually moving from the fringe.

Once the work of only "starving artists" who wandered into the art department or antisocial engineering types who toiled in obscure labs, design is now a prized skillset and sought after way of problem solving. Good design creates new opportunities that the traditional corporate hierarchy would miss or not take full advantage of, and this has the attention of even older, established industry leaders. That being said, this change can take years, even in today's rapidly paced business climate. Until a Masters of Fine Art is the common resume centerpiece of the world's top executives, young designers would be well served to understand business as it is now. This will help you not only work with "corporate types," but also communicate your value to each project and organization as you progress in your career.

Let us look at some common differences between formal business and the training of designers.

# Logic versus Emotion

DVD  Many sciences influence business training but none more so than economics. Economics, as it has been taught to business students for many years now, is precise and logical. There is supply of a product, and it can be assigned an algebraic variable. There is demand in the population for this product, and that can also be assigned to a variable. Thanks to this approach, supply and demand and any number of permutations and formulas that revolve around these concepts can be neatly calculated and entered into—every artist's favorite—the tabular spreadsheet to generate rather mundane graphs (see Figure 2–3).

Supply and demand is one of thousands of variables that businesses use to make decisions. The supply of data is endless. Studies and reports fill pages of charts and numbers to tell business managers around the world everything from the expected demand for premium fuel at a gas station in Miami Beach to the spending power of today's 10-year-olds once they reach the age of 25. Numbers and logic dominate business thought. There is a cottage industry of analysts and other number crunchers that supply this information to quench the insatiable thirst of business leaders for hard data—information they can count on, literally.

In walks the artist into this numeric mine field with an opinion phrased as "I think this— campaign, product, service, solution, color, pattern, music—will work."

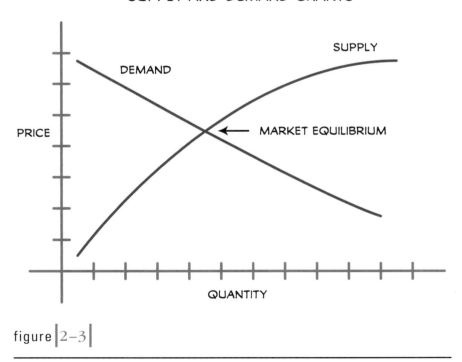

figure |2–3|

Economics and other core sciences of modern business training rely heavily on graphs and statistics, such as this supply and demand curve, to predict markets and make decisions.

Ultimately, the artist works on feelings and emotion, not just pure logic. Although many top designers will study market trends and other data, design is often not hard science. Design requires you to reach into the unseen and follow a path with few numbers to guide you. From the best advertising to the most sublime consumer electronics to automobiles that fetch thousands more than the cost of parts and labor could ever justify, design plays in a different arena than the comfort zone of most executives and decision makers in business.

How does the designer combat this focus on math and science with training in color and form? First, come prepared to any project, position, or presentation with what you want perceived as hard data. Don't have hard data on an ad campaign you just dreamed up while stuck in line at the bank last week? Find it. Find campaigns as offbeat as yours. Find products in other industries that tried the radical redesign you propose. Do your homework—and it will feel like homework— until at least some numbers support your conclusions (see Figure 2–4).

Second, make sure you keep your own accomplishments in numeric form. Did product sales increase 10% or 1 million units after you refreshed the design? Make sure you have that data. Did your last client have a 400% increase in lead conversion after the website was overhauled with your user interface work? Have that in your arsenal. Did the book you did the layout work for last winter set a record for sales? Add it to your credentials as why someone would *logically* hire you. Business runs on numbers and cold calculation, so make sure decision makers have at least your side of the story to plug in to their equations.

## TYPICAL BUSINESS PRESENTATIONS: STATS AND NUMBERS

figure 2–4

A typical business presentation is likely to use statistics and data instead of the emotional appeal of the arts.

At some point in your career, you may have reputation. You may be able to set the numbers aside and let your body of work speak for itself. Did you design the identity for one of the most-known firms in the world? Were the film graphics you designed the most imitated design element of the year—say, *The Matrix* titles in 1999? Did your copywriting spawn a million amateurs to post their own versions of your ad online—the "I'm a Mac." ad campaign of 2007, for example? At that point, your portfolio may not need to include stats. Until then, be ready to make a logical case for your work, even when you know it came from inspiration beyond trends and analysis.

## Profit versus Inspiration

The most maligned aspect of business is profit. Profit is invoked when critics of an industry or a particular organization want to call into question the motives of creating or promoting a product. Profit motive is often an easy target because, beyond some overreaching utopian goal of improving life for all humanity, profit is the reason for the existence of a business. There may be some inherent good created by the operation of a business, but without profit, the organization will ultimately close its doors. We will explore the profit equation later in the chapter, but for now it is instructive to understand that profit is the central goal of the business. The careers of many business managers rise and fall with only percentage changes in profit; profit is the bottom line.

Many designers, especially with a fine arts background, do not like their ideas turned into the simple Boolean equation of "Will this make us money, yes or no?" Artists work from a different perspective, and whether divinely inspired or just a *really* good idea, it seems callous and almost inhuman for management to boil the idea down to profits. As a designer, always remember that executive decision makers are first and foremost searching for profits—both long term and short term. If your idea, design, or solution is not going to make the company more than it costs to produce, in the worldview of business it should not be produced.

There are many, many great designs and great ideas that only see the light of day when they are found to be profitable. If you are certain your idea would make money but you cannot find an executive or a client who shares your enthusiasm, step back and look at the numbers they are using. Perhaps your idea is better suited for another firm, or could be produced with different materials, or would sell only in a given season and will take too long to prepare for this year's turn in the market.

Timing plays a big role in profitability also. The uses of retro and nostalgic images in advertising, for example, are usually reserved until enough time has passed that the negative memories of the era have passed. Use 1980s imagery in 1994 and the Cold War and corporate greed might be fresh in the public consciousness. Use the same 1980s images in a campaign in 2004 and customers would fondly remember a lighthearted era of synthesizer music and New Coke.

Regardless of what you need to change, a design that does not make a profit is destined to be a hobby, sideline, or never produced at all. For all the negative press corporations in some industries receive for record-breaking profits, remember that profit sustains the business and in only rare circumstances will management forego that responsibility to pursue your idea.

## Case Study: Lessons from the Pros: Addison Whitney

Numerous concepts will be well thought out, appropriate, and unique, but only one logo can be selected. Often it is not the most original or conceptual, or what is thought to be the best by the designers. Many business decisions effect the final selection, such as legal availability, senior management approval, and other outside forces.

Brinker International approached Addison Whitney® to aid in the repositioning of On The Border Mexican Grill and Cantina® to differentiate it from the Tex-Mex image of Chili's, a sister restaurant. Utilizing customer awareness and perception research of On The Border, Addison Whitney identified that the "sawtooth" design and the arched logo, possessed positive brand equity. Following a structured creative development and research process, Addison Whitney developed an award-winning design, which incorporates the sawtooth arch and associated vibrant colors. The lime wedge adds another fun element and immediately conveys authentic Mexican food and beverages, such as margaritas. The consistency of the colors and the sawtooth design are carried throughout the architecture and interior design of the new restaurants, further building the new brand identity (see Figure 2–5, Figure 2–6, and Figure 2–7).

figure |2–5|

Final identity.

Client: Brinker International

Project: On The Border Visual Identity

Creative Team: Kimberlee Davis (Creative Lead), Lisa Johnston, and David Houk

figure |2–6|

Final identity. "To Go" version.

Client: Brinker International

Project: On The Border Visual Identity

Creative Team: Kimberlee Davis (Creative Lead), Lisa Johnston, and David Houk

(a)

(b)

(c)

(d)

(e)

(f)

figure | 2–7 |

Sketches during the identity redesign process.

Client: Brinker International

Project: On The Border Visual Identity

Creative Team: Kimberlee Davis (Creative Lead), Lisa Johnston, and David Houk

# Repeatable versus Custom

Henry Ford is largely credited with the creation of the assembly line and the industrial revolution it spawned. The idea of diving tasks into small, repeatable steps so they can be duplicated en masse has since been at the heart of thousands of successful businesses in a variety of industries. Documenting every process from the 1 minute and 40 seconds required for slices of a potato to fry in hot oil to the scripted response a manager should follow to deal with an irate customer, modern business is designed around mass production.

Employees with similar skills can follow repeatable processes—even as one retires or quits or gets fired or downsized—and another steps in to work in their place. While this idea was originally conceived for the assembly line of turning screws and welding and stitching cloth seats together, the search continues for ever faster, more precise, more cost-effective ways to produce results evenly and predictably. The more processes that can be duplicated, the more costs can be lowered and profits can be increased. Mass production is efficient, and when a unit of the product you are creating must be duplicated, every aspect of its creation will be dissected and analyzed by management that is trained to understand and evaluate its suitability for the assembly line. The assembly line might be digital files that move across continents with a few clicks or actual manufacturing that will allocate resources at multiple production sites, but ultimately business must find a way to bottle success and duplicate it.

Artists then, by nature and training, do not look for such efficiencies and are understandably suspect when their creativity is turned into another cog in the wheel of a smooth running, mass production, business machine. Designers, especially before the reality of business sets in through the course of a career, often fancy themselves as artisans of a slower, more enlightened age. The creator sees the work as unique and timeless, not one piece in a million-unit shipment needed by next Thursday.

Although some design disciplines—especially industrial design—are taught to appreciate and work within the idea of mass production, many are still approaching design as craft. Craft and skill are certainly still important aspects of a designer's work, but business leaders who sign off on what goes from design to production are under constant pressure to produce more, cheaper, faster, and with greater efficiency.

How do you reconcile mass production with artisan care and craft? First, consider the influence and opportunity that mass production creates. Not every great work of art is a limited edition in a museum. Great music, for example, has spread far and wide to influence millions around the world because of mass production, mass marketing, and—at least until the digital revolution—mass packaging. The best music of the last century would still be as great without the mechanisms of business behind it, but who would have heard it?

Second, consider that not all mass production requires sacrificing what makes a design great. Thousands of niche markets are created each year and new manufacturing methods continue to reduce the scale of what can be produced for these markets. Although some industries—such as automobiles—have little room for niche design, even these old standard bearers of mass production have seen brands such as Mini and Scion offer endlessly customizable options and other makers latch on to the "mass custom" approach.

Embrace the constraints of mass production like you would any other design problem. Great design requires restraint; overcoming the barriers of a given problem creates the daily work of a designer. The identity package you create for a global client must have meaning in Beijing, Dallas, and Prague. Although this could be looked as a recipe for a bland, conservative mark that leaves nothing to chance, it could also create the opportunity to create something unique—and the fact that it is duplicated in any number of applications only further showcases the thought put into the work.

Finally, understand that business is not based on mass production by whim or careless choice. Business is under intense pressure to continuously lower costs and extract more from less. This goes from the raw materials of industry to the continuous battle among business competitors to attract talented people as employees. Employees—like you—have talent and skills and a unique approach that helps the business achieve its goals. But employees come and go for a variety of reasons, so the more a business can document and reproduce the results of their finest people—often called best practices—the less dependent they are on any one person in sustaining their success. The mass production process, even when applied to design and the arts, is there to extract the best you have to offer and multiply it by a scale that no single employee could match.

**DVD**

---

**Q&A Ask the Pros:**
**Organization and Details in New Hires**
**Alexander Isley**

*Q: Beyond a solid portfolio, what are you looking for in interviews with designers?*
*A:* Because our work has a spirit and sense of humor to it, for a long time I would get portfolios from the wacky guy or the class clown. But I prefer to hire someone who is more structured and disciplined because you can always get someone like that to loosen up. I think it is more difficult to ask someone more out there to become organized. So much of graphic design is working with clients and that is a really hard thing to teach people. People who work with me are detailed, oriented, and good at presenting their work.

---

## Numbers versus Images

Throughout this chapter, we noted that a good amount of business decision making was based on hard data—numbers. However, the tool kit of the designer—color, sound, form, shape, and motion—plays on the senses, not on the logical mind. This gives a designer a unique position in the organization as one that can alter perceptions, solve problems, and get across ideas without supporting evidence—without the numbers to back it up. This is a major reason why design has become the newest obsession of business leaders and why design training is so sought after in today's business world. Any number of professional specialties solves problems with logical approaches. If there is an existing case law on a subject, a lawyer can logically evaluate his client's approach to a suit. If the production capacity of a plant is at maximum and orders are still running late, operations can logically plan to expand. If the number means this, the logic speaks to what to do about it. But an artist works in the strange area around, beneath, and behind the numbers.

The conclusions of great design can often come seemingly from thin air—"More of our cars would sell if we offer this red I saw on a lipstick walking through the department store on Fifth Avenue yesterday." There is no evidence or any logical way to evaluate the validity of this opinion.

For this reason, business leaders are excited about the boundless opportunities present in the minds of their design staff and fearful that there is no way to extract such insights on demand or in a timely, efficient, predictable manner. You must keep in mind as you embark on your career that the training you have absorbed and skills you take for granted—knowing when colors look good together, seeing a typeface in your head that would be perfect for the campaign you are working on, knowing just when to cue the sound effects at the end of the opening credits—are not the domain of anyone else in your organization or the clients you serve. This is both a selling point and a detriment to your career. This is what you do and what you offer, but be patient with those you work with, because it is only part of a project to them. Most employees are not knowledgeable about design process and are counting on you to provide a perspective they cannot offer (see Figure 2–8).

## Factual versus Conceptual

A good designer is able to think conceptually. Using his understanding of a problem and all the variables that contribute to a given situation, a designer works with possibilities and ideas until a solution arises. This may happen immediately or in the middle of a meeting, but is just as likely to occur during a day off or waiting for a mocha latte during lunch hour. Concepts and ideas—and their counterparts shape, image, and color—dance in the mind of a creative professional and can be so vivid and all-consuming that the conclusions drawn have a powerful effect on the designer. The effect of all this natural, internal brainstorming is that the feeling that the idea—the solution he has in mind—is real, attainable, and correct.

Business though, does not work in only concepts and ideas. Business managers deal in facts. It is not a fact that your solution is correct. For that matter, much of what you use to draw your conclusion—influences that span your lifetime and shape your career—are not factual to an outsider either. Management is largely a practical, logical practice and not lost in the world of ideas.

This difference between conceptual thinking and factual basis for action must be understood to work in professional environments. The idea you have may be valid. The solution you dreamed up might be the right one. But a business is concerned with getting it right and taking the most direct route to a desired result. Your ideas are good when you have facts that back up your claim. Much like the weight given to numbers, the emphasis on factual information is not always appreciated by designers. Designers, as creative people, often have an aversion to taking facts at face value. If you create for a living, it is not a huge mental leap to think many truths are nothing more than urban legend or myth repeated often enough to take hold as fact. But while this may be philosophically interesting, your client or your boss is unlikely to take up the discussion. Instead of swimming upstream with a debate of what is factual or the value of your concept, find facts to back up your conclusions. A fact will often turn your hunch into something management finds actionable. A fact—"Sales of red cars were up over this quarter last year."—for example, will always support your case and gives business decision makers more comfort in dealing with a known—the facts—than an unknown—your opinion that a certain shade of red might work on this year's model.

J-LO MARRIED OJANI AND 21 MONTHS LATER DIVORCED HIM THEN DATED PUFF DADDY AND BROKE UP WITH HIM AFTER A GUN FIGHT IN A CLUB THEN MARRIED CRIS JUDD BROKE UP AND GOT ENGAGED TO BEN AFFLECK AND CALLED THE WEDDING OFF 3 DAYS BEFORE THE CEREMONY AND FIVE MONTHS LATER MARRIED SINGER MARC ANTHONY WHO LEFT HIS WIFE AND 3 KIDS AND NOW HE AND J-LO ARE REPORTED TO BE ON THE ROCKS. STILL WANT TO GET RELATIONSHIP ADVICE FROM THE ENTERTAINMENT INDUSTRY?

The glam world of entertainment is where we watch how life is supposed to be lived. But when we learn how to treat relationships as publicity stunts and meaningless exchanges, we're getting the wrong message. Entertainment is not real life. Don't get sold.

figure | 2–8 |

Client: Step Up Speak Out

Firm: Archrival

Creative Director: Clint! Runge

Illustrator: Carey Goddard

## Case Study: Elizabeth Arden Red Door Spas

# Designed by Alexander Isley Inc.

Creative Director: Alexander Isley
Managing Director: Aline Hilford
Art Director: Tara Benyei
Designer: Cherith Victorino
Designer: Hayley Capodilupa

We were approached by Elizabeth Arden Red Door Spas to develop an identity, packaging program, and communications materials for the launch of a new line of hair care products, to be called Portrait. The line would be positioned to women ages 30 to 45, a slightly younger demographic than Elizabeth Arden's traditional customers.

We began the assignment by developing a creative brief, in which we met with all stakeholders to further define the goals of the assignment. We then made a presentation in which we showed a competitive audit and analysis of the target audience: what she does, what she believes, and how she lives. We then presented a series of initial presentations in which we explored options for the packaging. Our plan was to show how the line was part of a system: how it was specially formulated and how it could convey a youthful and stylish spirit. We created a series of designs that used custom colors, patterns, and graphic techniques. Because of budgetary and time constraints, we determined that we would have to work with stock packaging materials, with the ability to specify only finishes and inks (see Figure 2–9 and Figure 2–10).

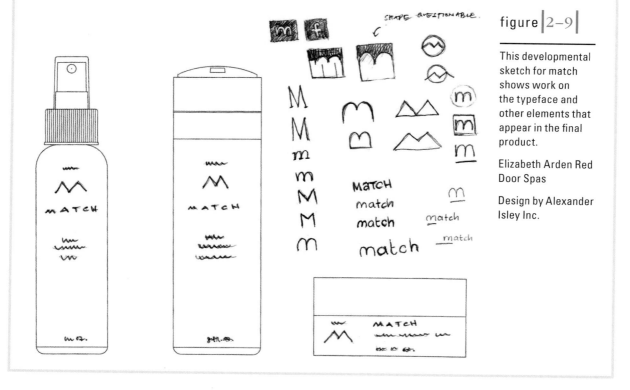

figure | 2–9 |

This developmental sketch for match shows work on the typeface and other elements that appear in the final product.

Elizabeth Arden Red Door Spas

Design by Alexander Isley Inc.

Alexander Isley Inc.

figure |2–10|

Developmental logo sketches for match

Elizabeth Arden Red Door Spas

Design by Alexander Isley Inc.

In our creative development, it became clear to us that the name that had been supplied could be improved upon, so we developed a series of alternate options. We ultimately recommended that the line be called "match," which speaks to the way in which the formulations can be tailored to different types of hair and combined with each other. This name fit the youthful and modern audience and the mission better and gave us the foundation on which to build the visual and editorial components of the brand (see Figure 2–11 and Figure 2–12).

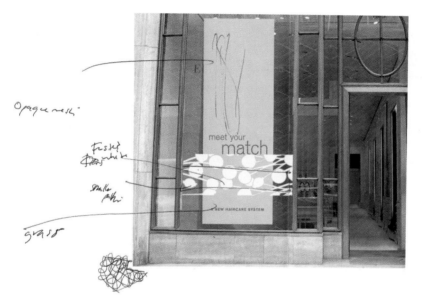

figure |2–11|

Developmental sketch for match, showing the entrance to the spa.

Elizabeth Arden Red Door Spas

Design by Alexander Isley Inc.

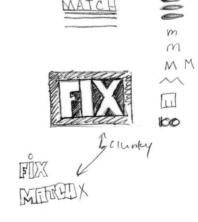

figure |2–12|

Developmental packaging concepts for match

Elizabeth Arden Red Door Spas

Design by Alexander Isley Inc.

The final design uses a signature blue-green color, custom made with pearlescent inks. The packaging incorporates a palette of natural patterns, suggesting variety within a well-considered system (see Figure 2–13).

Bag Sides

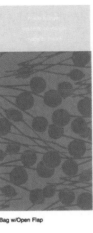

match

Bag Front

Bag Back

Bag w/Open Flap

Background

Foreground

Bag Bottom

figure |2–13|

Work on the patterns for the match packaging.

Elizabeth Arden Red Door Spas

Design by Alexander Isley Inc.

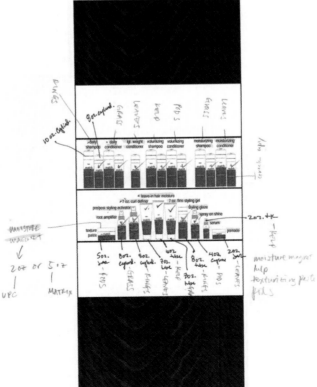

figure |2–14|

Shelf display concept for match.

Elizabeth Arden Red Door Spas

Design by Alexander Isley Inc.

The elements are used within all aspects of the brand's identity and communications materials: on the packaging, the brochures, on the website, on in-store merchandising materials, and on promotional mailings and bags. In addition to creating the visual materials, we were responsible for naming all of the individual units and writing the copy for the packages and the promotional materials (see Figure 2–14).

The line was launched with great fanfare and sales were strong. Based on the success of match, Elizabeth Arden Red Door Spas commissioned us to name and develop the look of mix, a corresponding line of products for treated hair (see Figure 2–15).

figure |2–15|

Final product, match

Elizabeth Arden Red Door Spas

Design by Alexander Isley Inc.

# Imagination versus Status Quo

The nature of business is conservative. Risks are calculated. Wild ideas are not acted upon with reckless abandon. Change is relatively slow and incremental. The best bet for this year is what worked last year. If the numbers show a trend that goes in one direction, all planning will be based on the idea of the trend continuing. Step one in the process should be followed by step two. Business courses are in large part designed around this conservative, timeless approach.

Little wonder then that the artist is left feeling a bit out of place. Groundbreaking art has always steered the opposite direction of the status quo. Creative minds naturally challenge the prevailing wisdom and seek new ways of doing things. Design is not at its most rewarding when the project spec is "add more green"—designers want to change things. Shake things up. Make something happen. Improve the human condition. Or at the very least, stop the use of such boring fonts in all their clients' sales materials. Although business is often the maintenance and protection of the status quo, great design often means tearing down what worked to build something better in its place.

Slowly, the business world is learning the value of such an approach. Designers are at the forefront of reshaping many industries around creating new markets and inventing entire new service lines instead of blind allegiance to what works right now. Business executives are looking for opportunities, as margins on old product lines dwindle in the face of global competition. The more whimsical approach of the artist, though still reined in by the inertia of business, has come to be more accepted and appreciated.

Although a grudging acceptance of this sort of creative risk taking is in vogue, the beginning designer will likely have to wade through many projects, clients, and even entire jobs that are based more on the work of the recent past and "what works" than any attempt at going in a new direction. Even in the most edgy, artistically free design shops, the bills are paid and the lights stay on because of rather mundane, routine, and unimaginative work that clients continue to request each year. If your dream is to redesign the Internet presence of Mercedes-Benz, you will probably find yourself making relatively small changes, minor updates, and occasional fixes to many unknown and sterile websites before such an opportunity crosses your desk. If you plan to design film graphics for Industrial Light and Magic, you may find that you will be learning your trade on local television ads or small national clients years before they need your skills.

The business of design is not always about creativity, but often it is about producing content. Thousands of annual reports, brochures, television ads, logos, websites, and other design work are constrained by conservative clients to be normal, even uninteresting, and only modestly different than the previous version. Learn what you can on each assignment and do your best work, understanding that the design industry is not always flush with requests for trend setting and avant-garde work.

# Long Production Cycle versus Constant Improvement

Most industries favor rather long cycles of planning a product, going through all the necessary contortions of development, testing, legal approvals, staff training, and other steps before releasing something new to the marketplace. Business fancies itself as fast changing and rapidly paced,

## Case Study: Sea Captain's House Rebranding

## Motto Agency, Inc.

Creative Team
Sunny Bonnell, Creative Director
Ashleigh Hansberger, Art Director
Kyle T. Webster, Illustrator
Design Challenge

Sea Captain's House, a Myrtle Beach restaurant, was built in 1930. In 1962, the property was sold and was to be torn down and replaced with a high-rise motel. At the time, however, financing was in short supply forcing a postponement of these plans. While waiting for the financial picture to brighten, the owners decided to operate the building as a restaurant. This planned year or two of waiting has turned into over 37 years.

The Sea Captain's House offers superb dining, ocean view, and warm southern hospitality. The owners called in Motto because they wanted their old "captain" to get an overhaul. The budget for this project was $10,000. We redesigned the captain by illustrating him with a modern twist and prepared redesigned captain for his glory days on a new apparel line for the restaurant (see Figure 2–16).

figure 2–16

The new illustrated brand of Sea Captain's House, Myrtle Beach, South Carolina. (Design by Motto)

but the reality of most industries is still that products take time to be developed. The larger the organization, generally, the more time involved in producing a new product. This relatively slow process means that there is a defined emphasis on getting it right. The product, after consuming the time and resources of the organization for an extended period of time, needs to succeed to pay back that investment. This level of pressure on each new product—or revision to existing products and services—tends to weed out many edgy, irrational ideas as too risky.

Designers naturally want to see their ideas come to life and get into the hands of the intended user or audience. The long—and expensive—production cycles of many businesses allow for only a precious few designs to go from concept to finish line. A shorter production cycle that gets more ideas out into the public eye would make the work of a designer, especially starting out in the business, more rewarding than spending months or even years on work that in the end does not make the cut. Although some design disciplines understandably take a long time to perfect, some areas of practice are starting to see continuous improvement cycles displace the harsh filtering of what gets released. In information design and interactive, for example, major international companies may still take months to design even small features for public use, but many more progressive clients are going in another direction. Instead of making sure every part of a design is perfect, they are releasing sites and site features much earlier in the design cycle and improving them based on user feedback instead of closed-door testing. This change of philosophy can be embraced by business not because of blind compassion for aspiring designers to see their ideas in public but simply because constant improvement is often faster and cheaper than long cycle development. Getting more ideas out in public sooner also spreads the risk of spending more time and money developing something the public does not want. The experience for designers of publicly failing—however harsh it might sound—can also be an excellent teacher when you know your next product will release in weeks, not years.

This approach has wide-ranging impact on business but obviously only fits certain situations. Ford Motor Company is not likely to skip their multiyear design and testing methodology to release fifty new models each year. Although that prospect might make the industry—and the public at large—buzz with excitement, concerns for safety and the price of ramping up an assembly line for each new model is prohibitively high to do so. Other market leaders in other industries use a long production cycle to make sure only the very best ideas of their design staff make it to production—even if it means hundreds of prototypes and mockups are thrown away to get to the very best the company has to offer.

The lower the cost of trying new ideas, the more likely the management might take the chance on a short production cycle. Your next idea for a video advertisement might not be green lighted for the Super Bowl, or even for broadcast on high-definition television, but thanks to the falling cost of technology, your employer may tell your team to shoot it and release the ad online or in other inexpensive video distribution arenas. This type of short production cycle was unheard of only a few years ago, and falling manufacturing costs continue to push the barriers of what can be produced with limited planning.

Cost and risk are always at the forefront of business decision-making, so understand that your client or employer is not intentionally moving slowly toward new products, services, or other market opportunities. If your ideas do not expose the business to legal problems and are inexpensive to produce, you might be able to persuade the executives to move faster and fix problems, make corrections, and add features as they arise.

# Business versus Job

Having a business and having a job is not the same thing. While this may sound obvious enough, make sure you have given some thought to the distinction when you are looking for career opportunities in design. Business executives are trained to create processes that earn a reliable, constant return on investment of capital. In other words, a successful business makes money for investors while they are at their desk, while they are asleep, and while they are vacationing in the Andes. This is a fundamentally different thing than a job, and most designers—and recent college grads in particular—are looking for a job. A job, no matter how sophisticated or how much training is required to perform it, converts labor into income. When you work, you get paid. When you do not work, you do not get paid. That is the nature of most employment, but not of a successful business. Many jobs mask this fact by offering salary, creating an illusion of income while you are, for example, on paid vacation. Salary can be a good thing, but it is still tied to performing a certain function for the organization.

Design jobs can offer secondary income in the form of residuals or royalties, but most work performed by starting designers does not offer this opportunity. Businesses do not approach earning money the way individuals do. When you design a product or a service, the business is looking for a way to earn money when you step away from it. The ad you create should return business to the client long after you have archived your Photoshop files and moved on to another project. The product you created should sell for some time after the testing is done and the approval is given to ship it. A business that does not earn money from past work is subject to continuously finding new clients just to keep afloat.

This distinction from earning money as an employee is critical to understand the rational of business executives. This is also important to consider when you plan to go on your own—see Chapter 8—and in looking at a client's ability to continually fund new work. Google, for example, ties an infinite supply of searches to advertising that is automatically placed by software that, while constantly improved, is already developed. Mercedes-Benz designers will spend years on a new product, but the product then can sell for a decade with only small, incremental improvements. This idea of earning residuals applies to Getty Images and their library of stock photographs or your local real estate brokerage and the percentage they earn when each agent under their employ sells a home. Business is about creating processes that generate continued profit. Jobs are created to fuel these processes.

# Risk and Reward

To understand how and why a successful business earns a profit, we have to look at the critical factors involved—time, resources, and risk. There are myriad other formulas for calculating profits, and we will even look at a few of them, but from your perspective as a designer, these are the main elements. A business invests the collective time of every person involved in the business, from the first paper sketches of the founder to the daily shift of the security guards. A business risks the time of their employees for the expected, or at least hoped for, result of profit. Time is the easiest to understand and appreciate, especially for many designers who hope to freelance or otherwise work for firms that bill their time to clients. Your expense of time is a primary component of the business.

A business risks other resources, as well. This can be a natural resource, purchased wholesale products that contribute to the business, digital assets, or information resources. A business acquires resources to risk them in the pursuit of profit. Looked at another way, if the resource is more valuable as it stands—money safely invested, employees working on routine takes, etc.—than it is to use on a new project, product, or service, the business is better off doing nothing.

That is an abstract way to view the allocation of resources but true nonetheless. It is most true of capital—monetary resources—the business has on hand. If a bank will give the business, for example, a 4% annual rate of return, and a new project that requires the use of this resource will earn 4% after all expenses are accounted for, the business will pass on the project because there is no additional return on the capital at risk (Figure 2–17). Each resource in the business is accounted for in this way. The work of the business decision maker is to maximize the profit from each available resource—including your time as an employee. This unfortunately means for many talented designers that their time is better spent, from the business point of view, on projects that are not high on the scale of interesting, challenging, or groundbreaking. They are projects that have the highest return on investment, and therefore are the most appropriate use of the designer's time at work (see Figure 2–17).

## BUSINESS THINKING: WORTH THE RISK?

CLIENT WITH $$ TO RISK

INVESTMENT ROUTE

4% RETURN

SAFE

SIMPLE

PROJECT THAT NEEDS
DESIGN HELP

HIGHER RISK

MORE COMPLEX

MORE TIME-CONSUMING

MUST RETURN MUCH
MORE THAN 4%, OR PASS

figure |2–17|

A business must determine whether available resources should be put at risk—developing new products, expanding operations, or even buying other companies—or should be left in safer investments that generate a steady return.

The business uses time and resources to earn a profit but only when it is put at risk. Risk is a critical part of the business equation. A business puts their resources at risk for the opportunity, the chance, that if everything goes as planned it will profit. An appreciation of risk, and your own tolerance for risk, will inform your career decision making in many ways. While many factors account for how much you earn in a career, the amount of time and resources you risk will have a direct impact on the opportunities, and as such, the income you receive for your work. Business successes make headlines, and the newest top selling product, top grossing Hollywood film, and fastest growing franchise might hide the casual observer from the fact that business is, at its core, a high-risk proposition.

## Risk Without Reward: Biggest Hollywood Losses

- *Battlefield Earth*—Cost $73MM, Earned $21.5MM
- *Waterworld*—Cost $175MM, Earned $88.2MM
- *Ishtar*—Cost $55MM, Earned $14.5MM
- *The Adventures of Pluto Nash*—Cost $100MM, Earned $4.4MM

(*Source:* BoxOfficeMojo.com)

## Risk Without Reward: Dot Com Failures

- Boo.com: Spent $188MM but was only in existence for 6 months.
- FreeInternet.com: Lost $19MM in one year (1999) before filing for bankruptcy in October 2000.
- Pets.com: Famous for their $1.2MM Super Bowl ad, they were listed on the NASDAQ stock market in February 2000 and liquidated 9 months later.
- TheGlobe.com: Stock shares traded at $97 during initial public offering are now worth less than 5 cents each.

Billions of dollars and millions of hours of labor are expended each year on products and services that do not earn a profit. This is the chance you take in business, and the reason executives are able to create a track record of success in creating profitable products and services are rewarded with enormous incomes and prestige.

The risk these business decision makers are taking is not, most often, of only their own time and expense. As often as not, it is not their own monetary risk either—at least not more than the value of stock and other investments. So who is risking everything to make all this profit? Investors. Before you write off investors as a small group of mega-billionaires, though they certainly do risk large sums in search of profitable enterprises, consider that millions of people take part directly or indirectly in financial vehicles such as the stock market. The global markets, which are hidden behind a wall of jargon and fine print in the retirement accounts of most workers, are the monetary resources used by many companies to risk for profit.

Let us explore an example of how resources and risk come together in a design transaction. An employee of a small local company invests a modest amount of money each month toward retirement. The money is put into stock shares of a larger, international company. This larger, international company requires an entirely new identity for a great product that is not making inroads with the target customer base. They call a design firm to do the work—your employer. After some negotiation, they hire your firm to do the identity work. The money they use, though passing through banks and brokers and all sorts of complex systems, is ultimately the money invested by the employee of the small local company. In this example, the employee is looking for a reliable return on their money toward retirement. The international company is looking for design work that helps achieve that goal. The design firm is providing the work toward that goal. The designer is employed to create the actual identity for the firm.

As you can see, the more put at risk, the higher the reward. The employee—by investing in a relatively safe retirement fund—is taking only a slight risk that their investment will be lost or will not return a modest gain. The international firm, by risking resources on a large scale must return a sizable profit. The design firm is risking the cost of employing designers and other staff without certainty that clients will continue to use their services. For this risk, they must earn a profit, as well. The designer, on salary, is only risking their own time, and that the paycheck from the firm clears.

Looked at in strictly monetary terms, a designer might be paid $3,000 for the month they are employed on the project. The design firm might involve two staff designers and a senior art director and earn the firm $20,000. The client, the international firm, might use the new identity system to increase sales of the product and earn over $1 million per year in additional profit for several years. The investor might never see a return directly from a single project, or even single company, but overall might earn 8% of their $2,000 investment in a year, or $160. This positive scenario paints a picture that the large firm is making an unreasonable amount of money from a designer that earned $3,000 for their efforts (see Figure 2–18).

Consider the same project, but the product does not catch on with the public and does not return a profit. Now the small investor, who has their monetary risk spread across many companies—each with a variety of products and services—will still earn their $160. Your design firm still earned their $20,000. Your paycheck still cleared. But the client is now out $20,000, plus all the time and resources of developing and marketing the product. In this scenario, the client is the one left feeling that other parties benefited while they did not. The business executive responsible for this project now goes from earning the company millions to explaining the loss of millions to upper management, the board of directors, and ultimately to the investors (see Figure 2–19).

This is the nature of risk and reward. Although obviously a simple example that leaves many variables out of the equation, the general principle is the same. Your design work, like the work of many others in the business world, is part of this complex system of risking resources for profits.

# COMPETITIVE ADVANTAGE

In the quest for profits, business must create and maintain a competitive advantage over their competition in the market. The customer base must deem their product or service better, for one reason or another, than something that can be substituted for it. In many ways, this is the reason for the business world's interest in design—creating an advantage through superior design is one of the primary ways successful businesses stay one step ahead. In this section, we look at some of the traditional ways business executives attempt to differentiate their offerings.

## A SUCCESSFUL RISK TRANSACTION

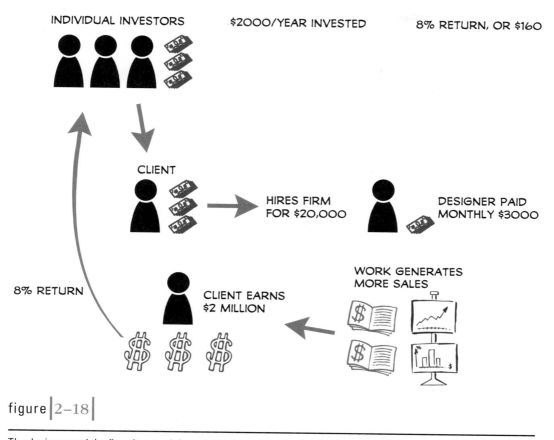

INDIVIDUAL INVESTORS   $2000/YEAR INVESTED   8% RETURN, OR $160

CLIENT

HIRES FIRM
FOR $20,000

DESIGNER PAID
MONTHLY $3000

8% RETURN

CLIENT EARNS
$2 MILLION

WORK GENERATES
MORE SALES

figure |2–18|

The designer and the firm they work for are hired on the basis that their work will return more to the client than it costs to have produced.

# Quality

Making a product of better quality can set it apart. That is simple enough in concept. An automobile that runs for 10 years without breaking down or a watch that ticks away without problem or clothes that stand up to years of use and cleaning will naturally be looked at, over time, as more valuable in the market because of their high quality. But to business, quality is easier said than done. There are several problems with basing your competitive advantage on quality, much to the chagrin of many designers who would prefer their work, once printed or manufactured or otherwise offered to the public, stands alone as the best. First, quality is only an incremental advantage. Management in almost any industry has to be too concerned with not just quality but perceived value from quality. If a competitive product is not poorly designed but instead only of slightly lower quality, the public—everyone except designers, for the most part—may never notice the difference. More importantly, they will not pay more for the difference in quality. This can be

## A RISK THAT FAILS:
## CLIENT LEFT WITH NO RETURN

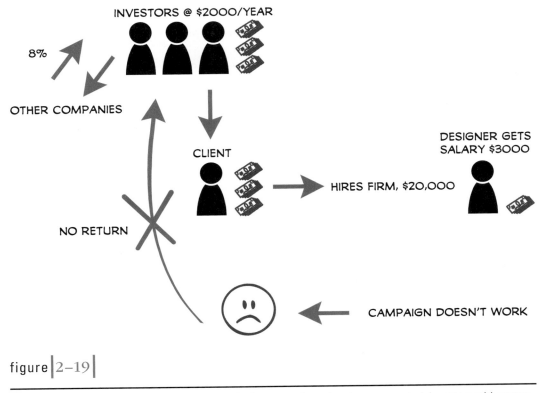

figure |2-19|

When a design project fails, the design firm and designer are often already compensated. Investors with money in various stocks will still average a return for the year, but the client is left losing money.

difficult to swallow for a designer, as the effort and attention spent on each detail of their work can wash away without notice when the customer is making a buying decision.

Second, quality is expensive. The higher cost of a product or service to produce will lower the profit unless the cost can be offset by more sales, a higher sale price, or both. The profit motive we already discussed can be a harsh judge of a design, as details that the designer would like to use—the better paper stock, the nicer cloth lining, a higher grade leather—can turn a product from profit to loss. This balancing act between high quality and low cost is the work of every designer and an inevitable part of almost any design project in any of the design professions.

Quality can certainly make a difference to the bottom line of a business. High-quality products can command premiums and cause consumers to go to extreme lengths to acquire them. But keep in mind as you work on a design that business views quality as a variable like any other aspect of a project. Be able to work at both the high end with the best materials and production options, but make sure your work can also travel down the scale—toward lower-quality materials and faster, less expensive production means—without losing effectiveness.

Quality is one way a business seeks competitive advantage. In many industries, offering second-tier quality at lower prices often will win business. The reality of business is that there is a market for products and services across the quality scale and the more of that scale you are able to work within, the more opportunities you will avail yourself.

# Cost

In today's hypercompetitive global market, lowering costs is a key competitive advantage for many industries. Cost, in the calculations of a business, has many variables and is not the same as price. The amount you will offer your goods or service to the marketplace is the price. The cost is the amount the company spends to create, market, and sell the product or service.

Your employers and clients are looking for a way to profit and have an advantage in the market, not just offer the lowest price. Your work as a designer is, more often than not, part of the cost of doing business. The value you bring to the business should be more than what it costs to have you employed. From a business executive's point of view, minimizing costs is a daily pursuit. Cost includes labor—your salary—along with raw materials, taxes, office and warehouse space, legal expenses, technology, and an array of other areas that must all be factored into the cost of a product.

Businesses are always looking for a way to minimize cost as a competitive advantage. Your design training can help this pursuit, as finding a better, more efficient way to do things is a natural part of your thinking and education. Find a way to use recycled materials if it saves money or use old layouts as a template for clients that cannot afford custom design every month. Save the company money—reduce their cost—and you are contributing to the bottom line.

# Distribution Network

Another competitive advantage is the distribution network a business uses to get their products and services to the end customer. This can be the elaborate network of trains, planes, and trucks of a global brand or just having the prime location in a busy corner of town. For new arenas such as digital media, the distribution network might consist entirely of hard drives and high-speed Internet lines. The speed, efficiency, and cost of getting the product or service produced, and in the hands of the customer all create a competitive advantage. This is a primary reason established companies in some industries see their advantage increase over time. As their network grows, it gets more efficient and less expensive per unit to operate. This makes it even more difficult for a newcomer to the industry to compete because they would have to overcome the advantages of the distribution network.

# Monopoly

Another advantage a business may have is monopoly power. A true monopoly—locking down an industry to just one company—is illegal in most capitalist countries. Too much power over an industry in the hands of one company creates abuses such as price gouging and also stifles innovation—why get better if there is no competition? There are many industries though that have product or service monopolies for a period of time. Because these monopolies control only small parts of large, complex industries, they operate legally and have become rather common. The competitive advantage of a monopoly is clear—if a company is able to shape consumer demand toward a product or service that they alone offer, they stand to make a profit from each transaction. Design can create and destroy this highly desirable advantage for a business. For example, a design that creates a new market segment can redefine the market to such an extent that all conversation, sales comparisons, and future product reviews are based on it.

## Innovation

When costs have been cut as far as they can be, quality is as high as possible, and there is no monopoly at work, a business can struggle to maintain its profits. This is the case in many industries each year, as intense competition drives down prices while not allowing for lower-quality products. For this reason, successful businesses are no longer solely occupied with maintaining their market share, but innovating. Innovation creates new markets and expands the opportunities of a business in ways that other competitive advantages cannot. When a business innovates, it offers something unique to the market, and therefore is less dependent—at least for a short time—on cost or distribution advantage. The iPod, for example, did not rely on price as an initial advantage. It was actually more expensive than other portable music players, especially the last generation of portable CD players. Apple has a mature, efficient distribution network in place, but could not rely solely on this advantage against consumer electronics makers such as Sony that are equally capable. The iPod was created as a high-quality product, but some areas were cost-prohibitive even at the time it debuted. For example, the design team may have preferred to use a color screen, but this was left out of the product until later versions. The iPod is an example of innovation. No other product had taken the idea of a portable hard disk that played music in the direction of the device, and consumers responded.

Starbucks, with its blended coffee drinks, was another innovative approach. Instead of competing with numerous coffee shops, diners, and restaurants with a product that has literally been offered for centuries—coffee—Starbucks created an entirely new class of beverages, from versions of Italian and French classic drinks to many new and infinitely customizable concoctions. The innovation, not the distribution network, cost, or existing monopoly earned market share. Now many firms are trying to compete with Starbucks by offering blended coffee drinks, but the innovation is lacking and they are primarily competing based on cost or other factors.

# THE PROFIT EQUATION

Profit, as we discussed in the previous section, is central to the ongoing success of any business. The standard equation for a business to determine profits is simply stated as—Revenue (the amount the business earned) minus Costs equals Profit. If the number is positive, the business earned a profit. If the number is negative, the business lost money.

But within this simple equation are many hidden details that paint a more complete picture of the quest for a profitable business. Focusing on design, the key questions for a business are as follows:

> • Is good design a cost?
> • Will good design earn additional revenue to offset the cost?
> • Can design save the business money in other areas?

As a professional designer, many projects you get involved in will have all three aspects to consider. How you relate your work to these parts of the profit equation will shape your career and the projects you work on. Let us explore the relationship between design and profit further.

Design costs money to produce. The salary or hourly wage of each design professional on a project is a cost of business. So too is the cost of the tools you use. You may have the impression from advertising and industry websites that all professional design is done on the very latest computers with the most up-to-date software, but this is simply not the case. Technology is an expense the business must account for like any other. Stock or custom photography, the use of freelancer artists, the materials of production—all are expenses. When you search for a job or plan to freelance, keep in mind that while your work may earn a substantial return for the business, it is initially an expense. When the business calculates the resources it needs to complete a project, expand their services, or respond to their competition, the amount you require to work for them is a cost. A successful business understands how to get the best talent to work for them in a variety of ways—from the environment they offer to the benefits they provide to the challenge of their clientele—but does not continuously overpay employees. It is not a personal preference or a mean-spirited human resources director who wants to negotiate down the last dollar when acquiring your services. Your income is part of the profit equation and, at least at first, a cost.

Once you are on staff or hired as a freelance worker, you have the opportunity to see your design skill turn your employment from cost to benefit. The first way this can occur is to produce higher revenue. When your design work can be shown to increase revenue, either directly—designing a product that sells big—or indirectly—designing an ad campaign that drives more sales, you are no longer just a cost of the business and the risk they took to acquire your skills has paid off as they anticipated.

The other payoff you can provide your employers and clients is cost savings. You can find where the business is needlessly spending money and reduce the expenditure. For example, a company may have a website that earns income but requires expensive staff to make changes every week. If you can redesign the site to reduce their cost of maintenance while maintaining other functionality, your design saves the business money and offsets your cost of employment.

 Your preference for applying design skills to these profit variables will start to shape your reputation in your career. Each area can be rewarding and pay well, so ultimately you need to determine what appeals to you about the work. Do you like the challenge of creating new products from scratch, something entirely new to offer the world? Or do projects like marketing and advertising appeal to you, applying your design skill to increase demand for existing products and services? Perhaps you see your best opportunity as a designer in redefining business processes to save your clients money. Designers naturally look for a better way to do things, but you have many options in how you direct this skill.

As you start your career, you may not always have complete control over where you fit in the profit equation. Project and job descriptions will often spell out what is needed, and your role is to respond to the needs of the business. This may be to find ways to reduce costs, to create a new product, or to generate demand for an existing product.

| | |
|---|---|
| **THE BOTTOM LINE** | • Business is driven by logical decision making. |
| | • No business can sustain itself long term without profits, and designers must understand how their work fits into this goal of clients and employers. |
| | • Business managers must find ways to replicate processes and products that are successful and not rely too heavily on any individual for continued success. |
| | • Business decisions are often made based on numbers and statistics and successful designers must translate their accomplishments into this form to communicate their value. |
| | • A business is based on creating systems to continuously make a return on investment, whereas a job is a trade between labor and income. |
| | • The time and resources put at risk in the course of business must return a profit much greater than safer investments. |
| | • For a business to succeed, it must find a competitive advantage over other products or services in the marketplace. |
| | • Innovation is a critical competitive advantage and an area that designers can have a significant impact. |

# THE JOBS

# introduction

When you leave school and join the professional ranks for the first time, there are a number of decisions that will shape your career. Your choice of specialization, or whether to develop a specialty, will narrow or broaden your number of opportunities. Technology will play a role in every design career, but the amount you rely on the latest tools or timeless principles will play a role in finding a job to fit your style and skills. One of the biggest decisions, and one that may be made based on opportunities more than preference, is whether to ply your trade at a large agency, a small boutique firm, or in-house for a corporate creative department. In this chapter, we'll consider these options and gain a better understanding of the jobs in the field.

# objectives

**Common job titles in the design field.**

**The difference between a specialist and a generalist, and how this choice affects your career.**

**How relying on technology or old-world craft can drive you career decisions.**

**How fine art and commercial art require different career-planning decisions.**

**The different types of employers in the field, from boutique agency to in-house creative department.**

# TITLES AND RESPONSIBILITIES

Leaving design school, you may have a lot of confidence in your skills. You should feel that way, as many of today's design schools are very proficient at teaching the practice of design. With all your talent crafted after years of study and assignments, there can still be a haunting feeling as you near graduation. The feeling can be best expressed as "Now what?" You finished all this training and are ready to turn pro, but you might not be exactly sure what an actual design job involves day to day. In this chapter, we review common job titles and the responsibilities generally placed on each position.

---

### Q&A Ask the Pros: Starting Out, Jon Pritzl

**Q: What was your title and what did they have you do in your first few weeks on the job?**
A: My title was graphic artist. I was pretty stoked to be part of an agency right out of the gates. The first few weeks were very exciting but also a bit intimidating. I was taught the agency's workflow and filing system. I was briefed more specifically on the client I was to be dealing most with. It was in these first few weeks that I realized there was a lot more to this job than just "cool design."

**Q: How was time allocated in your first year?**
A: In the first year of my job I would say that 80% of my time was production work handed down. After the sixth or seventh month, I started breaking into more direct client interaction and concepting some of my own pieces. At that point, I was able to speak directly with the client on ads and brochures to get their direct feedback rather than passed down through my art director.

---

## Production

Production work is not glamorous. Working at a printer or adding code to existing designs to make websites, though not going to win you an award, is good behind the scenes experience and where more than a few designers started out. The complexity of creating the finished products of design means production is not just an entry-level job either. Large publishing houses have specialists in the process of creating books and magazines, and modern production techniques can mean content is coming from databases and images from advanced asset management systems. Even if you do not plan to advance in production, it is helpful to know the pitfalls of creating the finished product and the entire process involved. For web and instructional designers, for example, the working knowledge of the easier programming languages, such as CSS and JavaScript, is crucial background before advancing to a design position that sends this task to specialists.

## Case Study: Vetrazzo by FINE

Image courtesy of Fine Design Group

Vetrazzo transforms recycled glass into artful surfaces for home or commercial applications including countertops, tabletops, and more. Core elements of the overall brand strategy developed with FINE are the distinctive Vetrazzo mark—a type treatment that echoes the appearance of the recycled surfaces—along with a Website that creates a venue for the narrative behind their products. Print materials and other outreach are in the works.

Vetrazzo

Creative Director: Kenn Fine

Designer (Identity): Clare Barnes

Designer (Web site): Jessica Christen

Image courtesy of Fine Design Group.

### Real Life Job Listing: Print Production Artist

### Description (excerpt)

You will gain valuable experience with a prominent and well-respected client and build your portfolio under the direction of an award-winning team of professionals.

### Essential Duties:

- Placing text copy with InDesign and/or Quark.
- Scanning, color correcting, and placing images.
- Prepare type and color release.
- New copy typesetting.

### Qualifications:

- BA in graphics or a related field with 2 to 3 years related experience, including related internship or freelance work.
- Advanced proficiency in InDesign or Quark. Skills assessment given before an offer is extended.
- Proficiency in Adobe Photoshop and Illustrator.
- Strong verbal and written communication skills.
- Strong organization skills and highly detail-oriented.
- Ability to multitask.

### What Do Production Artists Make?

According to the 2006 AIGA/Aquent Salary Survey, found online at designersalaries.com, print production artists average $40,000 a year in earnings in the United States. On the west coast, production artists averaged 10 to 12% higher than the national average. The median for the southeast states was lower than average but the same percentage. Keep in mind also that production is not always a junior position and the title of production artist at a firm that specializes in advanced print techniques could indicate several years in the field.

The 2006 Coroflot salary survey showed similar findings, but some respondents listed their position as entry level but salary hovering near six figures. There is always the exception to the rule, but there are also survey results that raise eyebrows. Asking for more than double the national average during an interview is probably not the best tactic.

# Staff Designer

The first time you are hired into a firm you could have many different job titles, but most of the positions are generally considered to be a staff level or junior designer. This role not only includes production work but also allows you to start doing layout, editing graphics, and helping out other staff as needed. There are two main areas of focus in a staff design position, and you must usually master both before moving up in the firm. First, you have to learn your employer's process. Regardless of whether your staff position is with a design firm or you are in-house at a larger corporation, your employer has a specific way of doing things. This includes everything from how to track your time to where to focus your energy when you have overlapping deadlines and every project seems to be coming at you at once. This can be a difficult time for new designers, as what you really want to do is show your skills. You will get through it, but you have to learn how the firm operates. It is very tempting to veer off into redesigning something that you are certain is so lame or ugly or old-fashioned that the client will love you for your efforts, but chances are this is not the case.

**Real Life Job Listings:**

**Junior designer**

The ideal candidate is enthusiastic about designing editorial columns and the front/back matter of magazines, possesses a willingness to learn, and accepts criticism well. The junior designer also supports the design team with components of feature stories such as drawing diagrams and maps.

**Primary responsibilities are as follows:**

- Work on the design of front and back of magazine stories.
- Assist in drawing diagrams and maps.
- Collaborate with photographers and editors to select images for stories.
- Assist on photo shoots.
- Support Production Manager with packaging and prepress issues.
- Maintain organized files of illustrators and other freelancers.
- General studio tasks.

**Specific skills are as follows:**

- Minimum 1 to 2 years experience or related internship.
- BA in Graphic Design or related discipline.
- A portfolio that illustrates a good understanding of grids and layout, and strong typography skills.
- Proficiency in the Adobe InDesign, Illustrator, and Photoshop.
- Good communication skills.

This leads us to the next role of a staff designer, existing projects. Although there may be employers in the world who will give their most challenging, interesting, and most high-profile work to designers straight out of school, the vast majority of assignments will be routine, even mundane work that just needs to meet the current standard for the client (or department). This can be very disappointing to new designers with visions of creating a new campaign for Volkswagen or turning out the edgy new layout for *ESPN Magazine* in the first year on the job. In most cases, you will have to slowly prove yourself and were probably added to the mix so the more senior designers had more time available for the high-profile work. Once you have learned the system, know what to expect of each client (and your management), and have worked on low level, off the radar work, you are ready to move up—or package your experience and move on to greener pastures.

### Time to Move On?

In previous generations, millions of workers worked for an employer the length of their careers. This obviously is not the same situation in most of today's workforce face, and designers can now expect to call several companies home—or at least call them work—before they hang up their Pen Tool and call it a career. How do you know when to move on? There is no standard answer, but a few clues can tip you off that the portfolio should be updated soon. Some employers do not have a broad range of what they offer to clients or what they require from their in-house design team. This is not to say the work is not good or even challenging, but it does mean you can expect more of the same. If you feel stagnant in your job and can see that senior designers have been in the same narrow range for years, you might need to move on to reignite your creativity. Once you have made a decision to leave and have a good certainty, or preferably written offer, that your next job is lined up, be fair to the employer you are leaving. So many firms merge and expand into other markets that you should at least state your interest to see if there is a match you did not expect. Perhaps you want to leave print production to do film graphics but did not realize the parent company is a strategic partner of a studio.

Connections and networking are vitally important in the design field, so do not just walk out in frustration and expect that employer will never know anyone else in the industry. Remember also that your coworkers and boss are in the same situation, and though your manager is unlikely to say "Leaving? Take me with you," it is entirely possible they will be calling you in a year for leads when they are ready to move on themselves.

# Senior Designer

Just as a staff designer may or may not have the title of Junior Designer, a senior designer is not always referred to by that title. In many cases, design firms are not that formal and simply being employed long enough and doing a good job will see your responsibility turn toward actively designing for projects. The role of more senior designers is what you might expect everyone in design does all day—the identity concepts in Adobe Illustrator or the image composition in Photoshop. The tools change, but in this role you are more likely to have notes from a client meeting and an otherwise blank sheet of paper. At this point you have the requisite background in dealing with production issues and an understanding of the needs of your intended audience but still actually design. At least in theory, you are still one of the designers and not in management, so while you may be asked to weigh in on a variety of problems, you probably are not responsible for hiring and firing and invoices and client complaints about other designers. This can be a happy medium for many designers, and as a senior designer you may find your niche area and develop deep skills in a certain specialty.

### Real Life Job Listings: Senior Environmental Designer

A [large city]-based graphic design firm seeks an experienced Environmental Graphic Designer to join our creative team. The environmental designer will work on a variety of projects to include wayfinding, signage, identity, print, and packaging projects.

We prefer candidates who have 5 or more years of experience with environmental graphic design. Candidates must have knowledge of fabrication methods, materials, and techniques and be able to take concepts through final production. Excellent communication, project management, and presentation skills are required. Must be able to work in a fast-paced environment and have a thorough knowledge of InDesign, Illustrator, Photoshop, and Mac platform.

### Do I Need Gray Hair To Be a Senior Designer?

The title of Senior might seem a world away from a recent graduate, but if you do good work and have talent, you may be there before the 60-month loan on your new car is paid off. Usually about 5 to 7 years of experience are listed for senior positions, but like any job description this is an ideal not a hard rule. If you have done top-tier work for 4 years, you are probably ready for consideration. At the same time, you could toil away in obscurity producing mediocre work for a decade or more before your skills are sharpened. The speed of your progression is obviously part talent, but there are intangibles to moving up including how much time you put in learning new skills and whether you have found the niche you really enjoy.

DVD

> **Q&A Ask the Pros:**
> **Getting Promoted**
>
> **Kim Davis, Director of Visual Branding,**
> **Addison Whitney**
>
> *Q: When do you know a designer is ready to move up to art direction or a more*
> *senior position?*
> A: When clients come to them for ideas. Clients will start to lean on a designer for their
> input on a project, often calling them directly, and I will notice that and see that [the
> designer] is ready for more responsibility.

## *The Down Side of Promotions*

An idea formulated in a book published in 1968 might not seem the best place to find career advice for the twenty-first century design industry, but *The Peter Principle* is still something to consider as you move up the ranks from staff designer to senior management. The principle states that each employee will rise to their "level of incompetence." In terms of a designer's career path, it simply means that a great designer—someone very competent—would likely be promoted to managing other designers (see figure 3–1). The promotion, usually given as a form of praise for good work, has the unintended consequence of moving the designer to a role in which they have no skills or training—a level of incompetence. Now the designer is removed from the work they excelled in—actual design—to a role they may not excel in—managing other designers. This promotion also guarantees that the designer will not be promoted again, as mediocre performance or poor aptitude for the new position will keep them from consideration. The designer in this scenario has already risen to their level of incompetence and is now stuck with a difficult choice of asking to be demoted back to the work they did best, investing time in educating themselves on management techniques, or changing employers before being shown to be incompetent.

Although this principle was spelled out 40 years ago, business continues to struggle with how to keep each person in a role for which they are best suited. It is natural to assume that a great designer will be even better when they run a team of ten or twenty designers, but this is a very different set of skills. Conversely, it is unnatural to think a designer with only modest talent would be effective managing a team of highly skilled specialists, but this can be the case. Effective organizations are able to strike this balance, but it is also up to you, as your career progresses, to be honest with yourself and your employers. Management can be rewarding and pay well but can also be a nightmare of bureaucracy and a world apart from creative work. Consider what skills you most want to apply before you inadvertently rise to the level of your own incompetence.

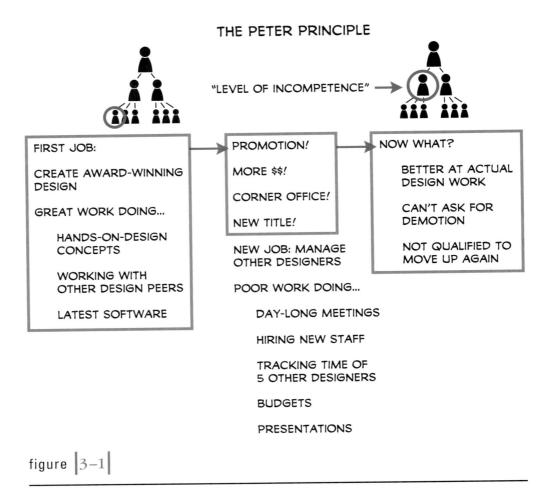

THE PETER PRINCIPLE

"LEVEL OF INCOMPETENCE" →

**FIRST JOB:**

CREATE AWARD-WINNING DESIGN

GREAT WORK DOING...

    HANDS-ON-DESIGN CONCEPTS

    WORKING WITH OTHER DESIGN PEERS

    LATEST SOFTWARE

**PROMOTION!**

MORE $$!

CORNER OFFICE!

NEW TITLE!

NEW JOB: MANAGE OTHER DESIGNERS

POOR WORK DOING...

    DAY-LONG MEETINGS

    HIRING NEW STAFF

    TRACKING TIME OF 5 OTHER DESIGNERS

    BUDGETS

    PRESENTATIONS

**NOW WHAT?**

BETTER AT ACTUAL DESIGN WORK

CAN'T ASK FOR DEMOTION

NOT QUALIFIED TO MOVE UP AGAIN

figure |3–1|

A designer promoted for doing great work may face the problem of being poorly suited for their new world of budgets, meetings, and managing staff, but unable to move back to daily creative work without asking for a demotion or leaving the firm.

## Art Director

In a small firm, an art director may work hands-on with projects and be the person solely responsible for creative output. In a larger firm or in-house creative department, an art director may have designers report to them and work in tandem with a copywriter. The managerial relationship of the art director to the team creates a new set of skills that must be learned. Art direction can allow the designer to get involved with multiple projects at once and work directly with clients more often. Because the detail work can be delegated to the staff designers, the art director is able to focus their attention on the bigger picture of a campaign or other creative project.

Although increased responsibility is often worth a salary increase—an average of about $10,000 over a senior designer—art direction is not for everyone. Similar to all your career decisions, you have to consider the role that you most enjoy and what direction you want to go personally. Any

**Real Life Job Listings: Art Director**

**Employer Description:**

We are a marketing consultancy that creates conferences, exhibitions, business-to-business events, launch events, ceremonies, public events, gala dinners, celebrations, receptions, road shows, and product launches.

**Job Description:**

- Qualified candidate must develop strategic b-to-b communications utilizing all applicable service offerings.
- Must work effectively with multinational clients and cross-cultural production teams.

**Responsibilities:**

- Responsible for the overall quality and originality of all communications services including 2D and 3D, interactive media, graphics, and live event solutions.
- Collaborate with account management and production teams to meet client expectations within budget.
- Contribute to content development, strategic planning, and proposal presentations.
- Educate, mentor, and motivate other team members.

**Qualifications:**

- An appropriate level of education, preferably in theater arts, communication, or design.
- Minimum 5 years industry-related experience.
- Proven leader, creative mind, and strategic thinker.
- Excellent interpersonal and communication skills.
- Good presentation skills.
- Enthusiastic and positive attitude.

director position that has other staff reporting to you will take time and energy away from the purely creative side of your work. A director must trade being closely involved with every detail of one or two assigned projects, for the opportunity to influence the work of their team. In the corporate world, many employees spend their careers always looking to move one more step higher on the organization chart. However, many smart employers understand the value of keeping each person in the role that fits them best, even if it means their senior designers might have more tenure and higher salaries than the people managing them. Some software companies take this to extremes, as senior staff with deep skills that are hard to replace might have millions of dollars in accrued stock options while their "boss" is still paying off school loans.

## Creative Director

In a larger organization, the art director often reports to a creative director. Although the titles are closely related, a creative director (also called a design director) has final responsibility for creative output of the firm. Each art director and their team report to the creative director. Another step removed from hands-on design, the creative director must focus on more high-level design and client relationship issues and not spend their time with granular detail very often. A creative director also has the task of setting the future direction for projects. For example, the creative director of an advertising firm would likely be in meetings with clients working on campaigns a year or more in advance of production. This can be a very interesting role but again depends on the personalities and preferences of the designer. Although creative directors have influence and input in a scope of projects unavailable to staff designers, they also have limited time to keep up with the latest techniques and tools of the trade. This creates a situation not uncommon in business that senior management—the creative directors and others with design or art background—may not be able to create their vision without staff designers. Every year the tools change and get more advanced, and the demands of business dictate that the more responsibility you will have in the organization, the less hands-on design you have time to do.

## Principal/Managing Partner

In many firms, the top of the organizational chart is the principal or managing partner. In-house creative teams might have a department head or Vice President of some kind instead, but the role is similar. For many top managers, design is background experience but not the daily work it was earlier in their career. The design work, viewed from the top of the firm or department, has to fit into the larger picture of running a business. While an art director might have several projects to get out, a firm principal is making sure that new work is coming in, projects are adequately staffed, and that existing clients are happy. The principal may certainly have more than a passing interest in project specifics, but their focus is on growing a successful business. Similarly, the head of a division of a large corporation may have a background in design, but their current responsibility is centered on the overall productivity and profitability of the division.

Each firm is different, but generally senior staff is responsible for selling new work. Although selling is not in the dream job description of most artists, new work is the lifeblood of the firm and plays an important role. There are firms that leave sales primarily to the sales team and allow the principals to stay actively involved in design. This requires a fairly design savvy sales and marketing group, as the intricacies of a project can have a large impact on pricing and scheduling. In either case, the top of the organization is likely to oversee other directors and managers and spend a good part of their day in meetings, negotiations, and other work that, though not design per se, is an important part of the industry.

## Real Life Job Listing: Creative Director

### Description

Your role is to establish and maintain the highest quality creative product. The Creative Director will coordinate and manage multiple projects from all stages of development from concept to final deliverable. This leadership role requires working closely with internal account managers and articulating overall direction for the design team.

### Key Tasks and Responsibilities:

### Creative and Strategic Function

- Provide creative leadership.
- Take responsibility for proposals, timelines, and production estimates.
- Develop and maintain client relationships.
- Ensure that deadlines and budgets are met.
- Develop an extensive network within the creative industry.
- Make presentations.

### Department Function

- Mentor, guide, and provide support for the design team.
- Encourage, motivate, and challenge the design team.

### Revenue, New Business, and Marketing Function

- Pitch development.
- Find revenue opportunities with existing clients.
- Lead development of proposals.

### Specific Skills

### Skills and Attributes:

- Strong leadership skills.
- Strong creative credentials.
- Exceptional communication skills.
- Excellent verbal and written communication, organizational, attention to detail, financial, managerial, and interpersonal skills.
- Comprehensive experience in producing creative.
- Ability to thrive in a fast-paced environment.

### Qualifications:

- Degree preferred or 10 years equivalent experience.
- Minimum 5 years experience in management.
- Travel required.

# TYPES OF DESIGNERS

Employers and clients can view artists more from stereotypes than work style. Some of this is not credible enough to delve into further, but there are a few important differences in approach and outlook between you and your fellow designers that are worth exploring. We want to look at the difference between generalists and specialists and how this can affect your career as you favor one path over another. Next, we need to understand how some designers rely more heavily on technology and some more on older, timeless methods. Finally, we want to consider how a fine artist might have a different preferred work environment, client, or project type than a more practical, business-minded designer. All of these groupings are not set in stone, and you could just as easily favor the latest software on one project and hand letterpress on another. In general though, these are natural tendencies that you want to consider as you map a career plan out for yourself.

## Specialist/Generalist

One of the primary differences between designers in terms of landing work and fitting into business assignments is how specialized they are in a specific skill. A specialist is expected to have deep experience in what they do. There are hundreds, if not thousands, of design specialties and each one answers a business need. Design software, for example, can spawn specialties by itself. Adobe Photoshop is a tool so widely used and has so much complex image editing capability that many designers achieve expert level in only one use or by targeting only one market. A specialist might base his or her career on editing images for the fashion industry. A keen eye for exactly how to get the most out of each image and a good understanding of what clients in this area require can make the job of a specialist very well defined. Someone using Photoshop for this niche would really know color adjustments and working with skin tones and hair at high-magnification level to make models look perfect and the products they represent sparkle. The same specialist might have little understanding of using Photoshop type features or using the vector tools to create a layout for a new website.

The advantage of being a specialist is that you can focus your efforts on putting out very high-quality work in your niche area. It allows the designer to block out much of the noise of the design business, as each new software feature or trendsetting style is only relevant as it relates to the specialty. The focus of a specialist equally applies to finding work and serving clients. Instead of marketing yourself as a "graphic designer" or "multimedia designer," creating your own niche can quickly communicate what you can do for the client. A business card and associated portfolio that shows you are a 3D motion graphics expert, for example, might get the attention of an art director with a need for this skillset on an upcoming project.

A generalist has a different approach. Instead of knowing absolutely everything about one specific area, a design generalist will have good skills in a variety of areas. A generalist might know enough Photoshop to edit images but not the subtle variations between how two fashion clients want their photos to look. A generalist might be able to do layout for a variety of projects and use type effectively but would likely use existing fonts and not create their own for a project. A generalist can be called on by clients or employers for a wide range of design projects and may work with specialists to finish fine details of a project.

# PHAT CHURCH
## A COLLEGE MINISTRY

Firm: LogoWorks

Project Description: Phat Church is a Christian ministry geared to the hip–hop generation. They describe themselves as "nontraditional, relevant, exciting, casual, and not boring." They expressed the desire to see ideas that would appeal to African-American college students.

## Special Concerns

Do not be too quick to declare yourself a specialist, and when you are ready to specialize, always remember that the design professions overlap and inform the work of each other. A specialist needs to have enough skills in related areas to at least competently work with other professionals. A specialist might hand draw the most sublime typefaces, but it will be prohibitively expensive for most firms to re-create that work digitally for use in their projects. A specialist also needs to be aware of changes in the industry, as their niche may disappear at any time because of changes in the market or in technology. This is especially true in web and interactive, as each new version of the leading tools reshapes the landscape of designers and developers, often automating or trivializing what was once considered high-end specialty work.

The advantage of a generalist is variety. There is no reason to get bored with a job description that allows every project to be different. As you start your career, you are often better off being a generalist until you find a niche you really enjoy. General design skills such as layout or illustration allow you to work with a variety of clients, and this can be a great exposure. Even if you specialize later, the contacts you make when you worked as a generalist will help you find work. In terms of job hunting and marketing, a generalist might have to sort through more listings and have a lower percentage of interested parties, but the number of available opportunities will be much higher. Some employers even prefer their new designers do not have a specialty so they can teach their own workflow and process.

### A Specialist Is Still a Designer

Design specialists are called upon for their skill, and often because such skill means increased speed to market. Just because you have become the world's foremost creator of stock illustrations of Victorian Era furniture does not mean a client will wait 6 months to see comps and may in fact expect your work faster than a competing firm. Some free-lancers also use their specialties in the wrong way by hiding from the realities of the profession. Spending 18 hours a day developing new skills can easily justify a lack of prospecting for new clients, but it won't pay for lunch.

The industry still is based, like any other, on time and money—delivering what was purchased on schedule and under budget. Firms use specialists to fill gaps in their own staff and strengthen projects, but that does not remove the designer from this equation. If your reasons for leaving a design position to freelance as a specialist include a disdain for invoices or deadlines, you may be disappointed to find out that you cannot avoid these realities of the profession.

### Q&A Ask the Pros: Hiring Specialists

### Paul Curtin, Eleven

*Q: What roles do you bring in freelancers or other specialists?*
A: We supplement our core with skills needed for a specific engagement. For example, if we have a project requirement for motion graphics, we might bring in someone temporarily to work at a high level in this area.

# Technologist/Craftsman

Another distinction between designers that can shape career choices is their use of technology to create their work. Technology plays a huge role in modern design, from digital illustration to photo editing to collaboration across continents. Design technology continues to evolve, allowing the work of one designer or small team to be replicated throughout an organization. This has not gone without its opponents though, and older, more traditional design techniques continue to appear as designers trying to create a unique look set their digital tools aside from time to time. For example, letterpress done in the traditional way created a great deal of buzz in the design community several years ago. Although, certainly, a look that digital design is able to replicate with some degree of success, the finished product was said, by its practitioners, to have a more genuine, authentic feel. Many designers are drawn to the old methods, from screen-printed posters to typesetting with actual lead because digital design techniques tend to catch on and spread so quickly that it becomes almost impossible to create something entirely new.

Other designers have the opposite view and appreciate the speed, accuracy, and efficiency that digital tools provide. There is also the situation of the designer learning the digital tools far in advance, and sometimes in place of, learning the underlying principles of good design. This can draw many more people to the various design disciplines that would never have otherwise pursued the career.

Your preference toward cutting-edge technology or old-world craft can help inform your decision making as you plan your career. There is room in the field for both approaches, and very few designers are exclusively one or the other. Even the most digital designer is likely to sketch ideas on paper, and hand-crafted design still might need email approvals or a promotional website.

Francis Ford Coppola's Rubicon Estate

Kenn Fine, Creative Director

Tsilli Pines, Design Lead

FINE Production Team

Coppola Art Department:

Gundolf Pfotenhauer, Art Director

As you look for employment, keep your own preferred work style in mind and you will have one more way to match your talents to your clients. Many employers will ask about your process for creating, as many art directors are leery of designers who rely too heavily on technology. Conversely, art directors cannot afford to add designers so obsessed with craft that they might miss opportunities to work more efficiently.

Designers who have natural talent in the arts often scoff at the idea of someone using limited skills and that a computer can compete with them. They would be better served to continue improving their own technology skills to supplement their talent and not wait for clients to appreciate talent alone. Remember that to a business speed, accuracy, efficiency, and cost are all part of what makes a designer or a design firm capable. Few clients will trade these traits, all of which are greatly enhanced by the proper use of technology, for pure artistic talent. Also be aware that design software, even your favorite tools, continuously adds ways to automate and duplicate design. The unimaginably skilled effect you just created for an ad campaign will be dissected by an army of technology hobbyists who will be able to offer the same look, but faster and cheaper, by automating the steps. Do not expect your talent alone to carry your entire career, and remember that design for clients is not meant to be great in a vacuum. Technology allows collaboration and communication like never before and closing yourself off to this as an artistic purist does not make good business sense.

---

**DVD**

**Q&A Ask the Pros:**
**The Importance of Visuals**

**Kenn Fine, Fine Design Group**

*Q: How do you get across to young designers that this is not just an artistic pursuit?*
A: It is tough, but I would bet if you made a top ten list of things that would most satisfy a client, I am not sure the look of the thing [the project] would be on it. So much more goes into the project. It is not just the artwork.

---

Some designers become so skilled in the digital tools that they feel anyone methodically creating a layout by hand must be out of touch or missed the bus to the future. Do not be so sure that real design skill is going away anytime soon. Although technology continuously changes what can be done, and how fast and cheap a certain look can be created, only with proper training and expertise in design can a unique, effective solution be created time after time. As an example of this, take the best technology person your design firm has and match them against a designer using old versions of software and old-fashioned techniques. You will likely find the new tools allowed a faster and incredibly precise design that is ready for conversion to hundreds of file formats. The older methods might be slower but often produce a more unique and original work that is grounded in timeless fundamentals. Continue to download plug-ins and keep adding memory to your computer, but do not convince yourself it will make you a great designer. Every few projects go back and force yourself to work on paper or with older coworkers to keep the design side of your skillset sharp as well.

# Fine Artist/Applied Artist

Although the distinction between a specialist and a generalist is important, other choices you make will shape your career as well. One such area is whether you considered yourself a fine artist. Applied arts are utilitarian and not intended for academic study. Although the emotional response of the viewer may be a result of the project, this is not the end goal of the work. Applied arts, such as almost all commercial projects, are meant to meet a business objective—driving sales, increasing brand loyalty, or reducing costs. Fine artists train for years to create their work, and generally do not have this same list of goals in mind. This can create a conflict between the artist and the firm that needs the artist. The business needs to apply art, whether the soundtrack to a new television spot or the imagery of a beautiful photograph, to a business problem. If you want to work as a fine artist and cannot see applying your talents for the mass consumption, capitalist, goal-oriented world of modern commerce, that is a choice you need to make. Understand though that your pure artwork, though not tainted by the hand of business, is also a much harder way to make a living. There is a reason that the term "starving artist" exists, and it is often not for lack of talent. Artists often cringe at the idea of using their skills to promote business, especially global brands, and frequently carry a political worldview that makes any work for these organizations an unconscionable act against humanity and not just an illustrated logo in four colors. The intricate conspiracies and urban legends that inform many fine artists could fill another book altogether, but ultimately the general sense is the same: business is evil and out to ruin the planet. This is a choice like any other, but as a professional designer, you have to reconcile the fact that your work is done for profit and that business itself is okay with you. A fine artist has a place in the world to inspire and create art for its own sake, and many designers create fine art on their own time. This is a different world than business though, and should be approached as such. If you allow your fine art skills and training to inform your design practice without putting an undue burden on each project to fulfill spiritual or creative outlets that commercial work is not suited for, you will be able to balance the two and can achieve success in both.

# THE JOB SEARCH

Creative work can turn up anywhere. From an innocuous conversation at a café to a call from an old classmate that has a connection, there are many roads that lead to a new employer. Although word of mouth and a good personal network certainly helps, there are resources that you can access yourself to make your search a bit less random chance. There are a number of quality sites online that can help you find design work as well as some firms that will place you with their clients in either a permanent or a temporary position. Of course, your own research should be exhaustive, and the old saying that finding a job is a job in itself is as true for design as for other disciplines. When it is time for an interview, you should be well versed on the past work of the firm or in-house team. You should come prepared not just with answers about yourself, your approach, and your work, but also with questions that show an interest in the firm and an understanding of how the job fits into your career plan. If you are interested in moving up and want to know about the track you would be on, interviews are your chance. If you would prefer to work in a certain specialty and shy away from presentations, an interview is your chance to match the job to your strengths and goals. Once you get the call, you have work to do to prepare to make your best case for being hired, but first you have to find the job.

# Staffing Firms

You might think of staffing, or placement, agency as more common in other industries, from day labor construction work to information systems. There are placement firms that focus a great deal of their effort on design work. These firms operate in a variety of ways and offer a range of services for employers from resume screening to background checks to full placement—including interviewing you at their offices before sending you to the employer for the interview. As a rule, these firms should not cost you to use, as the hiring employer is actually the client of these firms and pays for using the agency. An agency can be a great way to get into the door with hard-to-reach employers. Some employers prefer the screening process an agency provides and do not want applicants to call directly. An agency is ultimately a sales organization, and their role is to sell the services of talented people to employers. Once an agency has reviewed your resume, checked your resume, conducted an initial interview, and perhaps reviewed your portfolio, you can be assured they have a vested interest in your employment. Although many agencies work from annual contracts, the bottom line is the same—they need to fill job openings with talented, reliable designers. This is not to say that an agency will be able to guarantee you employment or you can coast on assignments because they will just send you somewhere else. These firms often charge employers hefty fees and expect results from anyone that is hired through this process. As such, the firm has to be discerning in their choices of designer, as their reputation is carried with the prospective designers they send to clients. Working with an agency can also be a benefit to freelancers, as many temporary assignments are passed to agencies to fill.

Some full-service agencies even have the ability to employ the designer directly, including benefits, vacation, tax withholding, and retirement savings, and then assign them to clients. This role fits between freelance and design firms, as the agency usually takes no active role in a specific project, but instead just sends designers as needed to work with an existing in-house team.

My agency disappeared, so now what? A placement firm assigned me to a client on a temporary basis. During my contract term, the placement agency went out of business, leaving my contract up in the air. The client still needed me to stay on the project, so we had to negotiate terms for continued employment directly. As it turned out, the placement firm was billing the client three times what I was earning—a formula that I would find out later is rather common. I was able to double my hourly rate at the same time the client was able to save money, so the placement firm was not missed. A full-service firm that offered benefits might have been more difficult to replace, but in this case the agency was simply providing labor and billing the hours so we were able to continue the project without much negotiation.

- Production work is good background experience and where many designers start their careers.
- The responsibilities of a staff level designer often include production work, but also layout, editing graphics, and learning the design process of the firm.
- Senior designers have the requisite background in production issues but work with clients directly and participate in conceptual work.
- Art direction can allow the designer to get involved with multiple projects at once and work directly with clients more often.
- The creative director (also called a design director) has final responsibility for creative output of the firm. Each art director and their team report to the creative director.
- A specialist is expected to have deep experience in a niche area that answers a business need.
- A generalist can be called on by clients or employers for a wide range of design projects, and may work with specialists to finish fine details of a project.
- Fine art skills and training should be used to inform design practice without putting an undue burden on each commercial project to fulfill spiritual or creative outlets.

# 4

MARKETING

# introduction

Design work is often closely tied to marketing and the related communications of a business intended to sell a product or service. This would lead you to believe that designers are natural marketers and that selling their services is the easiest part of the profession. Although some designers, especially those who work in advertising, certainly may understand how to create a campaign, an identity, or other sales collateral, turning the spotlight on their own services can make many freeze in a fit of uncertainty. When a designer begins to sell their wares as a freelancer or firm, the internal questioning and second-guessing starts—Whom do I sell to? What am I selling? Why do I need to market myself when I have so much work? How much time should I set aside to do marketing? Should my own marketing be my most cutting-edge, interesting work? Do I really need to call people or will my reputation carry me? Are not networking lunches and golf outings for bankers and other business types? Can I manage leads in Photoshop?

In this chapter, we take a look at what designers need to consider when marketing their services. Thousands of pages have been written on the subject of marketing. How to effectively sell, and the guru status ascribed to the originator of the newest approach, is always up for debate in a rapidly changing marketplace that has no surefire way to find clients. There are, however, practices that have held up more over time than others and are worth consideration. More than any single approach, from telemarketing to search engine ads to the local yellow pages, we want to explore the underlying process of finding a niche, understanding your potential client, and directing your energy in a focused manner suited to what you are selling.

# objectives

**Why unique market positioning is important to marketing your services.**

**The effect of location and travel on how your work is marketed and perceived.**

**What a vertical market is and how working in verticals changes your market positioning.**

**The importance of consistently prospecting for new work.**

**How to qualify leads before you have invested significant time and resources.**

**How to calculate a conversion rate to track your marketing efforts.**

**The value of repeat business and relationships in the design field.**

**How referrals can assist your marketing efforts.**

# UNIQUE POSITIONING

The toughest part of selling your own talents is understanding what you are selling. This process of self-exploration can take a few minutes for some designers and a lifetime for others. The skills you develop in design or art school can point you in many different directions, but only your own experience and instincts will determine the path you most want to follow. Once you have more than a vague idea about what you are best at and most want to do—or some comprise between the two—you will need to translate your offering into a unique selling proposition. This phrase, also known as a unique selling point (USP), or unique market position (UMP), means you must define how your offer is a better choice for your intended client than any other designer or design firm. Your unique selling proposition is a combination of the skills you offer, the payment you require, the speed of the work, and your own reputation. This is not a full business plan or a resume, but a short phrase or few sentences that will quickly communicate what you offer. Remember, the focus of your unique selling proposition USP is how your offer differs from every other designer, design firm, and agency the client will speak to about the same assignment.

> Your unique selling proposition must be very concise and easy to understand. For a company, this is often called an elevator pitch. The idea is that if you get on an elevator with a prospect on the tenth floor of a building, they know what your company does and how your service benefits them before they reach street level. Your personal USP should be similarly short and focused. If an art director asks you what you do, you have limited time to convey your skills and what you offer. Experienced designers develop this and when you ask them what they do, you generally get a short, precise answer—not an explanation of everything they have done in the past or hope to do in the future. Practice answering the question of what you do because when potential clients or employers ask you may have only seconds to communicate your message.

You want your USP to reflect what you do, but also serve as a guide in your marketing efforts (see Figure 4–1). If you have no unique position in the marketplace, why would anyone hire you? If your offer is the same as the firm the client just used, why would they use you? Although you may get in the door with your portfolio, to really make a career of design you must determine what sets you apart and market yourself based on this strength.

A USP also gives you a solid framework for projects. If your unique position is that you are the most skilled Flash animator in Atlanta, cutting your rate to win work from another person with less skill in your area does not fit your USP. Your relatively high price would be based on your assertion that if the client wants the quality you offer, it costs the few dollars per hour more than the lower-quality animator they interviewed.

Buzzwords come and go in every industry and design is certainly no exception. Although there is nothing wrong with using the latest terms to communicate your unique selling proposition, make sure you know what clients or employers will expect of the description. One example is *integrated marketing,* which is a very desirable skillset to many firms. While you may have, in fact, worked on the consistency of a branding campaign in school, using this term to explain your expertise in the industry would generally mean you understand and personally dealt with the political, communication, organizational, and cultural problems of branding across a large organization. It is always good to interview with knowledge of the latest industry terminology, but also be aware of what is expected before skills you have not acquired yet land on your resume.

## UNIQUE SELLING PROPOSITIONS (USPs)

GOOD:   ADVANCED DIGITAL COLOR CORRECTION, ———— (SPECIFIC, TARGETED)
SPECIALIZING IN FASHION,
SKIN TONES, AND LIGHTING.

BAD:   PHOTOSHOP AND OTHER ———————— (TOO GENERAL)
IMAGE-RELATED SERVICES

GOOD:   3-D MODELING FOR ARCHITECTURE ———— (SPECIFIC, TARGETED)
AND INTERIOR DESIGN

BAD:   GRAPHIC DESIGN FOR BUSINESSES ———— (WHAT BUSINESSES? WHAT
AREA OF DESIGN?)

GOOD:   IDENTITY AND PRINT LAYOUT AT LOW ———— (GENERAL SERVICES, BUT TWO SPECIFIC
PRICES WITH 48-HOUR TURNAROUND    SELLING POINTS: CHEAP AND FAST)

BAD:   PRINT DESIGN, WEB, VIDEO, ————————— (ALL-THINGS-TO-ALL-PEOPLE APPROACH)
AND OTHER DESIGN NEEDS

GOOD:   BOUTIQUE DESIGN FIRM OFFERING ———— (HIGH-END, EXPENSIVE, TIME-
HAND-CRAFTED INVITATIONS OTHER    CONSUMING, EXCLUSIVE)
FINE PRINTING NEEDS

BAD:   DESIGN TO FIT YOUR BUDGET ——————— (WHAT DESIGN? INDUSTRIAL? PRINT?
INTERIORS? WHAT BUDGET? $100?
$10,000?)

GOOD:   MOTION GRAPHICS EXPERT PROFICIENT IN FLASH, — (VERY SPECIFIC. RATES UP-FRONT.
AFTER EFFECTS, LIGHTWAVE, MAYA. WILL TRAVEL.    EASY BUSINESS DECISION: YES/NO)
$125/HOUR, OR $5000 MINIMUM PROJECT.

figure |4–1|

A good USP offers specific skills, often for a targeted industry, and at least an idea of costs to acquire the designer's services. Many designers want to keep their options open and by doing so create a USP too vague to quickly convey information to the busy managers and art directors who look to hire or outsource work.

For a designer with the USP that he can handle the most complex print work a client would ever need, politely refusing to redesign a website, would fit your selling proposition and strengthen it. If the designer swayed away from the USP and took the web job, he just moved away from a unique position and acted as a design generalist. That expanded the service offering but changed it from "high-quality print layout" to just "designer," and the marketing message conveyed to prospective clients would need to reflect this. In this scenario, the designer would be able to bid on additional web jobs, but also left an opportunity for another print specialist to service the client in that capacity.

Unique selling propositions must be understood from the client's perspective to be effective. Business decision makers use your pitch to understand what they are buying and frame the conversation and their expectation of your service around it. For this reason, your selling proposition must match what the client is offered. It is often tempting, especially when starting a career in design, to mold your pitch to the client in an attempt to sign the deal. Although this is certainly understandable, it is not the best strategy, as your client is not left with a clear definition of what you do and what you charge. It needs to come across in your presentation that you are a competent professional who has thought these matters out well in advance. We will review at length strategies for calculating billing rates and pricing your work, but the first component of your unique selling proposition is being clear to clients, prospective clients, and most importantly, yourself about what you offer the marketplace. If you do the nicest hand-drawn illustration the world has ever seen, you will find a market for your talent if you price and market your services correctly. It will not, however, be the same market that needs websites or brochures or any number of other design projects. If you see yourself as a generalist who can handle a variety of design tasks but not as a highly proficient expert on any one area, that is still a unique selling proposition and must be priced and marketed accordingly.

Client: Martini Racing

Firm: Damashek Consulting

A common frustration of business owners and managers is in knowing that they need expertise, but not knowing exactly who to call or what to spend. Your unique selling proposition must spell this out to the prospective client in a simple and approachable manner. If you do logos that take 2 weeks to complete and cost $1,100, that is hard data that a business owner can appreciate and make a decision on. Another designer might get nervous at their asking price or timeline and start to waffle and make changes in the middle of the pitch. Though well intentioned, this doubt can diminish the strength of what is being sold and cast doubt in the business manager's mind. Now two designers of equal talent are separated by their unique selling proposition. The one with a command of what they offer, how long it takes to do a job, and what they require per hour or per project will be more effective in the marketplace.

As an exercise, you should think through the variety of projects you have seen or worked on and decide how you would respond to these projects if they were requested of you (see Figure 4–2). The middle of a client meeting or presentation is not the time to decide on your service offering, pricing, or availability. If a client said, "I really like the logo you did, would you redesign the website?" Are you prepared with a response? Another client might like the brochure you designed, and wants you to do their Flash training modules. Is this an assignment you would want? Are you confident? How long would the job take you? It is okay to tell a client honestly that you will be happy to help them find someone to do work you do not do well or do not have as much passion for doing. The software you use likely does print, web, and even 3D and video equally well. But you must decide what *you* do, not just your tools.

## Soft Skills

We have already alluded to skills as being a primary component of a unique selling proposition. Being a print expert on a web job or a Flash coder stuck doing color separations is not what any designer wants. But these are not the only skills you need to consider when you define yourself for the market. The so-called soft skills, such as the ability to write or make presentations, also will define your offering. Again, you must be introspective and honest with yourself and determine your strengths and interests long before a client or an employer meeting. Soft skills can be developed like any other but also take time and practice you may or may not want to allocate. As such, interviewing for a position requiring a high level of personal interaction with clients is probably not the best role for a shy artist who wants to be left alone to create. The same role might be perfectly suited for an artist who gets creatively burned out by sitting at a desk all day and uses the back and forth of contentious meetings as fuel to keep pushing in new directions.

**Soft Skills are as follows:**

- Business Writing
- Presentations and Public Speaking
- Group Facilitation
- Consensus Gathering
- Mentoring

## YOUR USP MUST PREPARE YOU TO ANSWER A CLIENT'S REQUESTS

 CAN YOU DO IT CHEAPER? HALF PRICE?

 FASTER? HALF THE TIME?

 ALSO DO OUR WEBSITE?

 DO VIDEO GRAPHICS FOR TV? INTERNET?

 DO OUR ANNUAL REPORT?

 FOR OUR PARTNER BUSINESS IN ANOTHER INDUSTRY?

 WORK ON-SITE AT OUR OFFICE?

 WORK AT OUR OFFICE IN HAWAII? . . . IN JAPAN? . . . IN SAUDI ARABIA?

 CAN YOU PRESENT THESE TO OUR BOARD? FOR NO ADDITIONAL COST?

 CAN OUR STAFF DESIGNERS WORK WITH YOU TO SEE HOW THIS WAS CREATED?

 CAN YOU TRAIN OUR STAFF ON THE NEW DESIGN/IDENTITY/WEBSITE?

 WILL YOU WORK WITH OUR UNETHICAL/IMMORAL/POLLUTING/UNDER-INVESTIGATION DIVISION? FOR TWICE AS MUCH?

 CAN WE JUST USE THE PHOTOS/SOFTWARE/MUSIC/ILLUSTRATIONS WE FOUND ONLINE TO SAVE MONEY?

figure | 4–2 |

The process of creating your USP also helps you think through other questions a client or prospect will ask and have answers ready to go instead of improvising in the middle of a proposal presentation.

DVD

> ## Q&A Ask the Pros:
> ## Presentations Matter
> ## Ken Cook, Publicis & Hal Riney
>
> **Q: Aside from design and computer skills, what should a designer work on to be successful in the field?**
>
> A: Practice presenting. One of the rarest things I find is a designer or an art director who can actually command a room. To be able to stand up in front of a client and speak with conviction to the point that someone is going to take their money and pay you to do a project takes confidence.

Soft skills were overwhelmingly mentioned by designers and firm principals interviewed for this book when asked what they are looking for in designers they interview. Talent and portfolio was, of course, mentioned as important, but many firms place a high value on the ability to communicate in person, in presentations, and in writing. Clear, effective, error-free writing was mentioned often as a valuable but overlooked skill for visual designers. This makes sense, as promotions to art direction and management often require writing proposals and frequent written communication with clients, prospects, and partners.

# Location

It has been well documented that technology has collapsed many of the barriers of working across vast distances. While working in Venice Beach you can certainly save files on a server in Singapore for a client in London, but some work still requires proximity. For designers, especially in major cities, that could mean local or regional, clients are the best bet. It could also mean traveling to engagements, at least for a few meetings or photography or just to understand the local culture for the assignment. Your flexibility to relocate or travel is a question you need to prepare yourself for before interviews with employers or clients (see Figure 4–3). Many buyers of design are national or international in scope, and while that does not mean your first day out of school you will be on a plane to Tokyo or Cape Town, it does mean that you need to determine your own range before you Miss opportunities or disappoint a client that assumed you would be willing to relocate or take the "red eye" flight on two days notice.

Location has its perks, as long as you have thought through what you are offering and considered the effect on your value to the client. If you want to live in a more rural or unpopular area for design, your lower billable rate—driven by a lower cost of living—might be a serious competitive advantage against firms or freelancers from New York or London. The tradeoff, of course, is that you are not as likely to quickly become a big name in the design press or involve yourself in a thriving cultural community where your design talents might lead you into new areas. For some clients, the reputation of your big city firm is worth the additional cost, as having a logo by a known designer is akin to a painting by a past master of impressionism. To others, the work is strictly business and skills, turnaround time and price will drive the purchase decision, regardless of if your office is in Chicago's Printers Row or at your house in the suburbs of Buffalo.

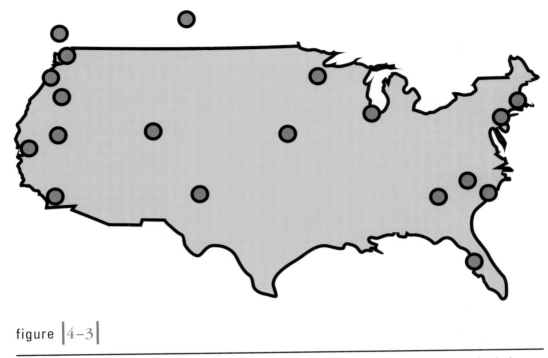

figure |4–3|

The designers interviewed for this book worked all over the United States and Canada, from the major design cities of New York and San Francisco to the small coastal town of Myrtle Beach, South Carolina.

The less tangible effect of location is inspiration. In speaking with designers across North America, many felt that the actual work created could be the same in a smaller town and great work would be recognized regardless of location. The same group, however, felt the larger cities, New York and San Francisco most notably, were simply better for designers because there is a larger amount of inputs from cultural trends, music, the performing arts, and other aspects of life in the city that keeps their work fresh. The answer given most often by designers who worked in larger cities was that the stimulus was worth the added cost of living and overall made them better designers than they might have been had they stayed away. Conversely, designers working in small towns and rural areas were intent on establishing their firms and chosen locales as on par with the design hubs and preferred their own work/life balance to city life.

### The Travel Advantage

When I left school, I worked for a well-known company in an unremarkable city doing work that was very leading edge and interesting. One of my best friends from school did the same work but traveled throughout the United States and occasionally overseas with a big name consulting firm. His salary was more than 20% higher than mine. The firm he worked for billed his time at roughly four to five times his hourly rate. His clients were in office parks around the world, and he usually flew in on Sunday and out of town on Thursday night. I did the same work in an office park in an unremarkable city that was a 1 mile commute from my apartment.

There is a difference in perception when travel is involved in a project. Fairly or not, rational or irrational, a higher value is often placed on talent that is brought in from out of town. If you fly in to work on an assignment, you are more expensive than your local counterparts. Be aware of this pressure if you take travel work, because all eyes in the office will be on you. Although business managers are unlikely to admit it, it is a natural effect of flying in talent is that they are perceived as more skilled and more worldly than local talent.

Think about the effect this has on your service.

"We brought in a designer based in St. Croix and a copywriter from an agency in LA to work on this campaign."

Or

"We brought in a team to work on this campaign. They have an office in that red building by the high school next to the mall."

Who has the higher billable rate? Who is better? It is impossible to say from just these two statements but also hard to argue that there is a distinct difference in how these two firms would be perceived, priced, and what level of work would be expected of their services. This is part of what you should consider when framing your offering, as local clients are more accessible, less expensive to establish a relationship with, and easier to find, but perceptions do play a role in how your service is viewed and what rates you can command in the marketplace.

# Vertical Market

Another differentiator for your design service could be specialized skills in a *vertical market*. The term vertical market is used to describe companies competing in certain industry category, such as entertainment or real estate or retail. By learning a significant amount about the workings of a certain industry, you can tailor your service offering to the clients or employers in this area. For example, your ability to create graphics and video presentations for trade shows could naturally lead you to specializing in this market. The trade show and convention business may need print and video work as other clients do, but as you learn the challenges and preferences of designing for exhibitors you will have an advantage over others without experience in this vertical.

Other common traits of clients in a certain vertical may have nothing to do with design but could be equally important in serving clients. Although one industry may be comfortable with prepaid retainers for professional services, another may be accustomed to another arrangement, such as Net 30 billing terms upon completion.

Another advantage of deep knowledge of a market is that the players within it often change teams. Your contact person at one pharmaceutical firm could be at another within a few months or years, and if a past experience working together was mutually beneficial, you may land a new client without ever calling them.

> Contacts are vitally important in business, and close-knit industries can amplify this importance. I worked in the corporate office of a fashion retailer and was surprised to find how many of our key staff had recruited each other from competitive labels. In such a scenario, your knowledge of the vertical market is not just design workflow but the tastes, habits, and personalities of the decision makers. These people may often change employers but stay within the industry. Your knowledge of the specific market then applies not only to your former coworkers but their new employers as well.

This is not to say that you cannot develop experience in multiple industries, and many designers do, but the intricacies of a market will not go into your proposals or presentations. Many markets that have long traditions and executives in these industries may not knowingly conduct business in a similar fashion but do so from years of ingrained business practices. Your experience with one client in the vertical will help mold your presentation for the next, until you are perceived as an extension of how they do business instead of an outsider. The same is true for interviewing for an in-house position because a job in layout for the publishing industry might have different demands than the same position in tourism.

## SALES FUNNEL

With your unique selling proposition ready for the world, it is time to start collecting clients. Whether a freelancer or a firm, the standard approach for turning leads into clients is the sales funnel. It is called a funnel because if you look at the process visually it is larger on top— the number of leads—and gets smaller as you get to the bottom—the number of closed deals. Understanding the sales funnel is critical to your marketing efforts for several reasons. First and foremost, you will be able to see the relationship between leads and sales, and this will give you much better idea what a lead is really worth to you. Second, the funnel will remove the false (but very common) sense of security that a month or two of being "very busy" with client work can create for a designer. The funnel is not a strict set of rules—you may need 10 or 1,000 new leads to get ten new clients this year—but it is a good approach to learn until you really have a good understanding of the sales process. The process that creates the sales funnel is fairly standard for most professional services. From design to law to computer repair, a professional needs to first prospect to new clients. A prospect creates a lead, or a potential new client. A lead can become, depending on your process, a presentation or a written proposal—and often both. A proposal in writing can be signed as a binding contract for services, and traditionally this is the end of the funnel.

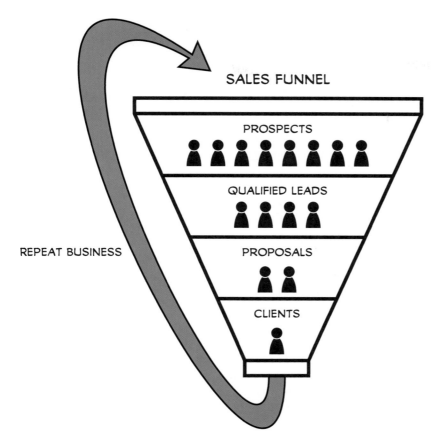

figure |4–4|

The sales funnel is used to track how many prospects, qualified leads, outstanding proposals, and new clients are currently in contact with the firm.

Successful professional services businesses understand that the end of the funnel is not only projects but also repeat business. Repeat business, a satisfied client who generates a new project, means that the top of the funnel is not just prospects and that new work can come in without constantly converting new leads (see Figure 4–4).

# Prospecting

Prospecting is the art (or perhaps, science) of sifting through thousands of businesses and selecting the few that are legitimate leads. There are many methods to prospecting as there are prospects, so unless you plan to make a career exclusively of sales you will want to select a few and get better at them. Some methods are impossibly easy to understand and get started. For example, cold calling. All you need is a phone book and a phone. Call a business and solicit them for design work. This is not the most efficient way of doing things though, and you could waste the first year of your career trying to get a project in this manner. As such, more sophisticated prospectors use list services and other methods to narrow down the list to likely buyers.

## Case Study: Archrival Gets Their Start

As told by Clint! Runge

This is one of my personal break out projects. The owner of this carwash had shut down for 9 months while he completely renovated the machinery. After closing for that long, of course, he had lost all his loyal customers. He was looking for somebody to do a newspaper ad to announce his grand reopening. His budget was $1,200—which does not get you much in terms of newspaper advertising (see Figure 4–5).

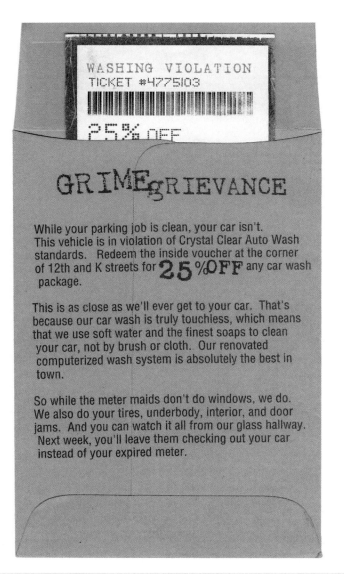

Image courtesy of Archrival.

I told him we could do more with his $1,200 than a traditional newspaper ad. He was open to ideas. I said let us do something not so traditional—this was before this sort of thing was super popular. It was the early years of Archrival. We would go on to build a reputation around this sort of nontraditional thinking.

We decided to "ticket" dirty cars in the downtown area (the carwash was the only one serving the downtown area). To pull it off, we did some intensive research to try and figure out how to mimic the City of Lincoln parking violations material. After some phone calls, we finally found where the iconic pink envelopes were bought from (somewhere in North Carolina). We bought a lot of envelopes, printed up some tickets, and put some funny headlines on the envelopes (see Figure 4–6).

WASHING VIOLATION
TICKET #4775103

**25% OFF**

TICKET #4775103
Date: 1/29/00
Time: 17:30

LICENSE: couldn't see it

STATE: NE
EXP. DATE: 2/29/00
VIN:
VEHICLE: DRTY CR

VIOLATION: DIRTY AUTO GRIEVANCE
PARKING: YES
METER #: 0505

**FINE: 25%** OFF
ANY CAR WASH PACKAGE

TOWED AFTER 15 DAYS OF BEING DIRTY
LOCATION: 12TH AND K STREETS
K-1-2

*PLEASE RETURN TICKET WITH REDEMPTION*

figure |4–5|

Image courtesy of Archrival.

We dressed up and began our mission. When we found a dirty car, we would give it a ticket. Sometimes we would stick around the corner and watch the person's reaction when they saw they had a ticket. They could not believe it. They would check the meter. There was still time on it. Oh, can you picture the reactions! People hate getting tickets, but man, when they saw they still had time on the meter they were priceless (see Figure 4–7).

Of course, once they inspected the violation they realized the joke was on them. Inside was a ticket worth 25% off a carwash. Many people laughed and put it on the car next to them or on a friend's vehicle (see Figure 4–8).

Now here is where we took this concept to the next level. We flooded the local newspaper parking lot with these tickets. To our luck, two people actually showed up at the City of Lincoln Violations Bureau to pay for the ticket. Of course, the parking people have the humor of about a brick. They called the sheriff. Chaos ensued.

All of this landed the tickets on the front page of the *Journal Star Newspaper* the next day. And what did the article say? Sure, it talked about the fake tickets, but it was mostly about the new Crystal Clear Carwash. Once the newspaper did it, local TV was not far behind. They all wanted in on the local interest story. The car-wash was flooded with cars and the local TV stations got some good shots of it (see Figure 4–9).

For what was originally going to be a $1,200 small little newspaper ad, we turned it into a direct mail, front page, 60 second prime time local news ad campaign. The moral of the story? Problem solving gives graphic design the opportunity to become something special. When you are early in your career, you have to look for the right times where you can do something more. As I said, this laid the groundwork for more local work (see Figure 4–10).

Name _____

Address _____

City _____ State___ Zip_____

PLACE
STAMP
HERE

Crystal Clear AUTO WASH

After a $5 parking ticket and a $75 tow, you're gonna need a break on a

car wash.

figure |4–6|

Image courtesy of Archrival.

figure |4–7|

Image courtesy of Archrival.

figure |4–8|

Image courtesy of Archrival.

figure |4–9|

Image courtesy of Archrival.

figure |4–10|

Client: Crystal Clear Carwash

Creative Director: Clint! Runge

Designer: Ryan Cooper

Firm: Archrival

Using cold prospects, or businesses that have never heard of you, your business, or your work, is a difficult road. As such, warmer prospects are always what you are looking for, and that starts with your personal and professional network. Communicate what you do to everyone you know, first, so you avail yourself to as many warm leads as possible. It is much more effective to call your uncle's best friend or your roommate's boss about a design assignment than starting from scratch with no ties and no relationship in place. This is true in prospecting for full-time work or clients, as this is often the same phone call with temporary assignments leading to interviews for staff jobs.

A common mistake made by designers starting out is being reluctant to talk about business. This comes not only from the "artist" role in society, but also from a natural aversion to this kind of thing. To many designers, being a salesperson and prospecting for clients conjures images of cigar-smoking industrialists of yesteryear or 1980s bond traders having a laugh on the fairway at the country club. In reality, everyone with a job works for either a government agency or a business and needs that entity to be successful to maintain their employment. Your work is important in the marketplace, and you are not offending sensible people to say what you do and ask for a name to call. You do not want to be overbearing or too forward with your personal network, but you must also remember that you must find employers or clients to do what you presumably love to do—your design work. Prospecting is simply narrowing the list of businesses from, for example, the Google search result when you type your city to a manageable list with a higher probability of using your services. Many marketers insist that prospecting is more attitude than anything else and see the world as full of opportunity at every turn. You do not need thousands of prospects, even when running a large firm, therefore you can afford to be a little more selective than if you were selling say, magazine subscriptions by mail. But you still need a large enough pool of prospects that you have a good number for the next phase of the funnel, the lead.

## Leads

So you have narrowed your list of businesses and included every business that your personal and professional networks suggest you call about an opportunity. You are ready to send proposals now, right? Unfortunately, no. The prospect is the top of the funnel, and you now need to qualify the lead (see Figure 4–11). A qualified lead means that the business meets a few criteria. First and foremost, they must be interested in a project that you can do. This returns us briefly to our discussion on unique positioning. If you call a prospect and they are very excited to sign a design proposal that does not fit your offering, it is not a qualified lead. You must move on. That does not mean you cannot assist their search or even refer them to colleagues, but they are not currently qualified to be your client.

Next, they must be able to pay you. Although it is generally a matter of tact not to blurt out "Can you afford me?" on the phone, you must have some idea that the prospect in question understands you are professional and a bill must be paid for work to occur. There are various approaches to this, and the appropriateness of each is often tied to the size of the client. Larger firms will have their own credit rating, and more likely than not you will also be able to track down some other vendors—payroll, information technology, the cleaning service—who could attest to their ability to pay on time. For smaller clients, the decision maker might be an owner and your assessment of their financial ability will come down to trust. This is another reason that prospecting by professional network is preferred to cold calling. Your professor, another client, or a former coworker is unlikely, at least knowingly, to refer you to a nonpaying client.

## QUALIFYING CLIENTS

**READY.**

IMMEDIATE NEED?
LONG-TERM PARTNERSHIP OPPORTUNITY?
USED CREATIVE FIRM BEFORE?
NEED SERVICE THAT MATCHES YOUR USP?
GOAL IN MIND—INCREASES SALES, REDUCE COST, NEW MARKET, ETC.?

**WILLING.**

IS WILLING TO BREAK FROM CURRENT DESIGN PARTNER?
USES PROFESSIONAL SERVICES INSTEAD OF HIRING IN-HOUSE?
SEES DESIGN AS A COMPETITIVE ADVANTAGE
WAS REFERRED OR WANTS TO UNDERSTAND YOUR WORK AND PAST
PROJECTS

**ABLE.**

CAN AFFORD SERVICES NEEDED?
DID NOT BASH LAST 2 OR 3 CREATIVE FIRMS?
SCHEDULE AND TIMELINE EXPECTATIONS FIT WHAT YOU CAN PRODUCE?
AGREES TO STANDARD PAYMENT TERMS—NO SPEC. WORK

figure | 4-11 |

---

Asking the right questions can help you quickly determine whether a prospect is a qualified lead and potential client.

There are other considerations to qualifying, such as timeframe—can you do the project if they need immediate turnaround?—and location if that is relevant to the assignment. You should always feel like you have asked enough questions of a prospect that you would be comfortable working with them. It is not necessary to dwell on the negative of a prospecting call—every client could be scrutinized until faults appear—but you should be conscious of your gut instincts also. Were the answers correct but something was just not quite right in the conversation? Did you feel like the prospect got uneasy when you mentioned a deposit for work to commence? Was the prospect's criticism of their last freelance designer baseless or unreasonably harsh? You must keep in mind that while you may, at times, just need an assignment to pay the bills, the bulk of your time working on the sales funnel should aim for long-term clients.

## Conversion Rate

Your conversion rate is used to keep track of your marketing efforts. This is a simple measurement, usually expressed as a percentage that is derived from dividing the number of leads by the number of new projects. Thus, ten leads that turned into three new projects would be a 30% conversion rate. Conversion rates vary from firm to firm or among freelance specialties, so this number is really a monitor of your own efforts more than a barometer for you to compare yourself to other designers.

If you are selective with your clientele and take a limited number of projects per year, you will likely have a much lower conversion rate than a designer who will do logos for $300 on a one week turnaround. Even knowing this, you will want to track your conversion rate over time to monitor your marketing efforts. For example, a conversion rate of 100% might sound perfect, as every lead is turning into new work, but it could also mean you are grossly under pricing your time compared to other designers with the same talent level. The more leads you have, the more meaning you can glean from your conversions, and there is certainly an element of trial and error involved in adjusting your services to meet market demand (see Figure 4–12).

## CONVERSION RATES

### EXAMPLE 1: SKIPPING TO PROPOSAL STAGE

| PROSPECTS | 10 |
|---|---|
| LEADS | 8 = 8/10 = 80% CONV, PROSPECT TO QUALIFIED LEAD |
| PROPOSALS | 7 = 7/8 = 87.5 % CONV, LEADS TO PROPOSALS |
| CLIENTS | 2 = 2/7 = 28.5 % CONV, PROPOSALS TO CLIENTS |

TOTAL CONVERSION = 2/10 = 20%

RESULT:

IF EXAMPLE 1 INCREASES THEIR PROSPECTING WITHOUT CHANGES, THE FIRM WILL SPEND MORE TIME WRITING PROPOSALS THAN BILLING HOURS.

IF EXAMPLE 2 INCREASES THEIR PROSPECTING, THE FIRM SHOULD GROW SLOWLY AND EVENTUALLY BE ABLE TO USE REFERRALS TO INCREASE THEIR CONVERSION RATE.

TOO LOW.

PROBLEM EARLIER IN FUNNEL OR PRICING DOESN'T MATCH EXPECTATIONS.

TOO HIGH.

NOT QUALIFIYING HARD ENOUGH OR ASKING ENOUGH QUESTIONS BEFORE PROPOSAL STAGE.

### EXAMPLE 2: EFFICIENT FUNNEL

| PROSPECTS | 10 |
|---|---|
| LEADS | 5 = 5/10 = 50% - HALF ARE QUALIFIED, HALF ARE NOT |
| PROPOSALS | 2 = 2/5 = 40% - PROBABLY ACCURATE, 2 OF 5 HAVE IMMEDIATE NEED THAT MATCHES OFFERING |
| CLIENTS | 1 = 1/2 = 50% - LESS NEW WORK THAN EX. 1 BUT PROBABLY 1/3 THE TIME PROPOSING TO UNQUALIFIED LEADS |

TOTAL CONVERSION = 1/10 = 10%

figure |4–12|

Understanding your conversion rate, or the percentage of leads that turn into signed projects or clients, will help you find problems in your sales funnel and allow you to generate more business.

Within the conversion rate, you should also track the steps of the sales funnel to see where your marketing is going wrong and where it is working. For example, you might have 100 leads in a month and of these, thirty are qualified. These thirty qualified leads result in ten presentations, or 33%. Of these ten presentations, nine firms request a formal proposal. On the surface, this 90% rate would seem to show your presentation is working. The final step, going from proposal to signed project, might fall to 1 of 9, or just over 11%. This low closing rate would lead you to rewrite your proposal. It could, however, also tell you that your presentation and proposal are not working together. In this scenario, you would want to revisit your presentation, even though it appears to work, because it may be making promises—even by implication—that your proposal does not fulfill. Perhaps your presentation refers to a low price you offered another client on a much easier job. This would set a false expectation, causing clients to request a written proposal in hopes of hiring a low bidder. This would fail when your proposal arrived and your actual rate is in writing. Thus your proposal might be fine, but needs to be teamed with a presentation that more accurately reflects the costs of a project. This might lower your conversion of presentations to proposals from 90 to 30%, but raise your final conversion rate from 1 of 9, or 11%, to 2 of 3, or 66%. This would ultimately mean only one additional project of the original 100 leads, an increase from 1 to 2%, but also results in having to generate fewer proposals. This is an important savings of time that could be used to work on other aspects of your business or find more leads. Study your numbers at each step of the sales funnel and look for reasons why each qualified lead did not sign for new work. This will help you narrow down the problems with your offer and make your overall marketing more effective.

# RELATIONSHIP MANAGEMENT

Having looked at the sales funnel, we can reason that keeping the top of the funnel filled with new leads is critical to the long-term success of a freelance designer or creative firm.

Equally important to new leads is generating additional work from existing clients. Building long-term relationships with clients is both mutually beneficial and much more cost-effective than working on single projects.

Managing the relationship with the client enables a designer to work on additional projects as they come up without a lengthy proposal cycle. Trust established during an annual report project, for example, could easily lead the client to call when they need an identity for a new product, an ad campaign, or other needs. Business decision makers would generally prefer to work with their creative firms for a longer period of time, as the process of finding and selecting a firm is long and expensive. More than just cost though, the long-term relationship between designer and client enables more strategic planning and consistent handling of the brand. Brand management, as a natural outgrowth of design work, is increasingly important to business. Each use of the names, logos, colors, slogans, and products of a firm must be considered for how it fits the overall message that is communicated to the public. As such, the television ads, Internet sites, signage, uniforms, company vehicles, and any other asset of the firm must be consistent. Each of these projects generates additional work for the firm, but because there is an established relationship, the cost, speed, and quality of the finished product should all improve when compared to using a new design team on each.

# Repeat Business

DVD For the design firm, client relationships generate repeat business and are the lifeblood of the operation. Although a firm should not rely too heavily on any one client, most firms do have a core of clients who have new projects on a fairly consistent basis. This is important to realize as you look for work, since the core clients of the firm will largely determine the projects you can expect. If you have your heart set on cutting-edge work but the clients are blue suit banks, the firm may not be a good fit. On the other hand, if you want to learn the studio system and develop a good understanding of process, the same firm that works with conservative clientele might be an excellent opportunity. Make an effort to understand the work being done by the firm, both current and past, and ask questions about the clients. A creative firm that has partnered with a client for years may be trusted to take the brand in a different direction, so do not write off the traditional clientele of some firms as boring. The staid old airline industry, for example, once relied solely on images of their largest jets soaring across the sky to a dramatic music score. That was before Southwest Airlines changed the business and now run national television ads featuring suburbanites throwing produce, among other amusing creative hooks.

Because the creative firm is often tied to a select group of clients, it is important to understand the broader industry in which they operate. Principals and creative directors throughout the design business stress—often repeatedly—that understanding the bigger picture and not just the actual art is critical to success. Your client will look to you for ideas and solutions to problems, not just very skilled Photoshop work. Your solutions should be informed by your deep knowledge of the previous design projects of the firm, the current and past work of competitive firms, and the overall picture of where the client fits—and has the greatest opportunity—in the marketplace. This understanding, and how it can effectively be applied to the challenges of a client, is a key reason why the long-term relationships enjoyed by many studios exist. Rather than waiting for a new studio and its designers, directors, and project managers get up to speed on their industry when each new problem arises, a business decision maker may find it must easier and more cost-effective to lean on their creative partners for years.

The long-term client is a balancing act on the part of the studio. Although critical to consistent revenues and long-term planning, the same familiarity that allows the firm to develop deep understanding of the client industries can generate predictable, uninteresting design that is ultimately ineffective in the market. In this situation, the client may actively seek out another firm to look at problems from a fresh perspective and without preconceived ideas of what will work. The business decision maker has to weigh the known, predictable work of their long-term creative partner with the new, but unproven, ideas of another firm. These decisions can change the course of businesses—both the firms and the clients—and the careers of the creative professionals involved.

# Referrals and Reputation

Referrals can drive the success of a creative firm. Ironic as it may be that some of the best advertising and graphic design groups in the world do not advertise their own services in the traditional manner; reputation can bring in more work than even the best campaigns (see Figure 4–13). Word of the mouth in the creative services is strong and though the influence and exposure of the work is

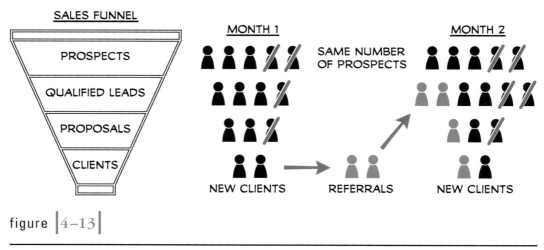

figure |4–13|

Referrals and reputation can drive more business than other marketing efforts and reduce the amount of prospecting required to be successful.

great, the actual number of accomplished practitioners is few. Buyers of design, such as marketing managers and other business executives, are often not trained in the arts and will rely on the opinion of designers they trust to find other specialists. Likewise, these same decision makers can have their careers and reputations greatly enhanced by the astute application of design to their business problems. Finding creative professionals can be very difficult and time consuming for executives, and they may continue the relationship with the designer or firm even as they change employers.

DVD Your reputation as a designer, and more so as a business problem solver, is one of your most important career assets. Design is often a reputation business, and many of the firms we spoke to in preparing this book were able to initially build on the reputation of the partners.

- You must determine what you uniquely offer the marketplace—your unique selling proposition—a combination of skills, costs, speed of delivery, and reputation.
- The standard visual representation of the process for turning leads into clients is the sales funnel. The funnel is larger on top—the number of leads—and gets smaller as you get to the bottom—the number of closed deals.
- A qualified lead means that the business must be interested in a project that you can do and both willing and able to pay for the work.
- You should always feel like you have asked enough questions of a prospect that you would be comfortable working with them.
- Building long-term relationships with clients is both mutually beneficial and much more cost-effective than working on single projects.
- Long-term clients are critical to consistent revenues and long-term planning for design firms but over time can generate predictable, uninteresting design that is ultimately ineffective in the market.
- As a designer, your reputation is one of your most important career assets.
- New firms often rely on the reputation and previous work of founding partners to establish their client base.

# PROPOSALS
# AND PROJECTS

# introduction

How much should I charge? If there is one question that design students repeatedly ask themselves—and ask peers, instructors, even parents and friends—it is the basic question of pricing their work. There is no simple answer, since the cost of design work is as varied as the work itself, but in this chapter we will explore the most common methods a design project progresses from initial contact to actual project.

Once the design firm and client agree on the project, there are myriad deadlines, phone calls, and e-mails to manage. In the second section of this chapter, we will look at project management techniques for creative work.

# objectives

**Design is a professional service and charging a reasonable fee is appropriate.**

**Your work should not be overpriced because you distrust business, see your work as fine art, or feel your work is the same as larger budget projects.**

**How to set a rate by time and materials.**

**How to set a fixed price for a project.**

**How to set a per diem, or day rate.**

**Why billing rates are so much higher than hourly wages.**

**What common project deliverables and assumptions go into a proposal.**

**How to manage timelines and dependencies in a project.**

**How to use change orders during a project.**

**When it is appropriate to vary your pricing.**

# CHARGING FOR YOUR WORK

Students of design and the arts commonly struggle with pricing their work. This usually manifests itself in two ways—wildly overpricing their work as if it was museum-ready art or grossly underpricing their efforts to the point that taking a client feels more like graphic servitude than a career. Both situations do not benefit the designer or the client; therefore, we must first address the general idea of setting a price for design before we explore the various methods to create an agreeable rate.

We will start by getting this out of the way—as a commercial artist, a graphic designer, or another of the various titles you may give yourself, it is okay to charge a fair price for your time and effort and the skills you have developed. At such time that your skills have developed to the point they are ready for application by business—presumably during your years at school—you have earned the right to consider yourself a professional and provide a professional service.

A doctor is paid for his knowledge and how he applies it to a problem. A lawyer is, as well. You are trained in the graphic arts to use these skills to creatively solve some of the most demanding and difficult problems a business faces, those of communicating a message clearly and effectively. Unlike many other professionals though, many artists do not view their skills in this way and become uneasy about charging for their time. For many, their core talents in drawing or use of color are innate, and though years at school may have sharpened their skills, it is still something that feels very natural to do. This natural ability shields artists from one of the truths of the profession—that not everyone can do this work. Successful designers understand they provide a service that, when executed at a high level, takes as much work, talent, and practice as the other, more traditional departments of a business operation such as accounting, finance, law, or sales (see Figure 5–1). So that said, there is a basis for charging professional fees. If you are serious about a career in design, you must appreciate that you add value to the business by solving a problem, and this justifies your fee.

On the flip side of this equation are artists with little or no professional experience that have an inflated idea of the value of their work. This may come from a general distrust of business or some other internal agenda to avoid clients, or may just be the runaway ego fed by the status of being the best illustrator at a given college or most skilled layout artist in a small town. So yes, some corporate identity projects do run into the six-figure range. It is also true that your client does stand to make hundreds of thousands or even millions from their business operations. It is also true that great art can, as it stands alone to be one of the finest examples of an era or movement or technique, command huge amounts for gallery exhibit or at auction. None of this has anything to do with your graphic design work in the first few years of your career, if ever, and should not inform your pricing when you leave school.

The large budgets of corporate identities, first of all, are set as such to pay for teams of experienced professionals to research and dissect every corner of the market. They must take into account everything from how the new identity will be viewed in many cultures to scaling the identity from business cards to commercial aircraft fleets and cell phone video ads to display screens at Yankee Stadium as 40,000 fans wildly shout around it. The scope of the project is one factor, but there are many—including legal issues with every similar mark in use, present or past, and of course how competitors with similarly huge budgets are branded globally. Your work, alone, is

## PROFESSIONAL SERVICES

| | QUALIFICATION/ TRAINING | BILLING METHOD | OTHER INCOME | TYPICAL COST |
|---|---|---|---|---|
| LAWYER | LAW SCHOOL, BAR EXAM | RETAINER, HOURLY | SETTLEMENTS | $$$$$ |
| PHYSICIAN | MED SCHOOL, BOARD CERTIFIED | CASH FOR SERVICES, INSURANCE | RX SALES | $$$$$ |
| DENTIST | DENTAL SCHOOL, BOARD CERTIFIED | CASH FOR SERVICES, INSURANCE | ADD-ON SERVICES, SUCH AS WHITENING OR ORTHODONTICS | $$$$ |
| DESIGNER | ART SCHOOL OR SELF-TAUGHT | RETAINER, HOURLY, PER PROJECT | LICENSING, STOCK ASSETS | $$$ |
| MECHANIC | TECH SCHOOL OR SELF-TAUGHT, CERTIFICATION | PER HOUR OR PER JOB | PARTS, WARRANTY WORK | $$ |
| PLUMBER | TECH SCHOOL OR SELF-TAUGHT | PER HOUR OR PER JOB | PARTS, WARRANTY WORK | $$ |
| LAWN CARE | SELF-TAUGHT, TECH SCHOOL CLASSES | PER JOB OR MONTHLY RECURRING | LANDSCAPE PRODUCTS, TREE SERVICE | $ |

figure |5–1|

Professional services vary in terms of the expertise offered, but they are all based on the idea of charging some amount per hour or project for the application of specific skills and training.

one part of this massive effort for projects of this size, and therefore not the basis for dollar figures that make headlines in the design and advertising press.

Your client may profit from your work. As mentioned earlier in this volume, this profit motive is not to be disregarded. Profit is not optional to a business, and should not just be a pleasant side effect of your labor. The client must find profitable solutions to their problems to continue in the marketplace, and you must be comfortable with this idea to work in graphic design. Setting an obscenely large price for your work will generally keep you out of the market, and though there are guidelines for using the revenues of a client to estimate pricing, it is based again more on required research and project scope and not on distain for corporate profiteering or some feudal attempt to get even with an established capitalist enterprise.

The last common cause for overpricing is the idea that your work should be priced as art. Although you may do fine art for a client, it is applied to a business problem and is therefore a commercial work. Your client is unlikely to engage in a discussion of what your work is *really* worth, in terms of contribution to society, but only assign a value based on their own business needs and how this commercial art helps to that end. If your work truly is valuable to the art community at large as fine art, that is a separate pursuit with its own methods of pricing and negotiation and operates with different demands and expectations than commercial work.

# Time Tracking

The price of a professional services engagement is based on the number of hours of skilled labor applied to a given project. This number of labor hours may be spelled out directly to the client, along with an hourly rate, or it may be only part of a calculation done internally by the management of your firm. In either case, time is a critical variable to the cost of a project, the revenue of the creative services firm, and the income of the designer(s) on the project.

One of the more difficult aspects of the transition from school to the design industry is the emphasis on delivering work fast and efficiently. Unlike a school project that might allow several weeks or months and add up to hundreds of hours, clients will require much quicker turnaround. As important, the firm must account for the time of each designer and cannot afford to allow projects to use more resources than was budgeted.

To further understand this, let us look at a simple example of how pricing for a creative job might work. A design firm may charge, for example, $100 per hour of work. Their proposal to the client might be $10,000 to complete a project. This means that only 100 hours ($10,000 divided by $100/hr) of work are scheduled to complete the tasks of this project. Although 100 hours might seem to be a good amount of time, these hours can quickly expire and must be budgeted among the various tasks of such a project.

The key thing to understand is that time spent on a project is integral to the business of creative work, and one of the key differences between fine art and commercial work. Although a world-renowned masterpiece of painting, sculpture, or music might take years to achieve, commercial work must be completed in the tight schedules of business. Therefore, the key to doing great commercial work is thriving under constraints such as costs, deadlines, and client objections. While many artists can create when given as much time as they need, top designers and design firms understand they do not have this luxury and there is always compromise to meet the conflicting demands of great design and fast delivery.

In the following section, we will see how time—both billable time and the hours clients will not directly pay for—is kept and turned into the cost of a project.

# Rates versus Wages

Billable rates for freelancers tend to be much higher than the hourly wage of an employee doing the same job. This is very attractive to many designers, especially as they first leave school, and the idea of earning $50 or $75 or $150 an hour seems a world away from the meager existence of their current job. Before you jump into freelance though, it is helpful to understand the key differences between a billable rate and an hourly wage. What you may find is that the economics does not always favor the freelancer, so this career choice should be made based as much, or more, on factors such as your tolerance for risk, your ability to motivate yourself, and how comfortable you are marketing your skills to clients.

Client: Burnet, Duckworth & Palmer LLP (or BD&P), a Calgary-based law firm. Design by Sasges Inc.

As an example, we will compare a $40,000 per year job to a freelancer billing a rate of $50 an hour (see Figure 5–2). On the surface, the $40,000 per year job pays significantly less. If you first divide the earnings of the employee, $40,000, by the number of hours worked in a year, 2,080, you get an hourly wage of only $19.23. Conversely, if the freelancer were able to bill 40 hours a week for a year, their total income would be at $156,000—almost four times the amount the employee earns! This is not the whole story of employment though, so before you rush out to print business cards let us look deeper into this scenario.

To be a freelancer, you must do much more with your time than design. Although some client meetings or travel time is generally billed to the client, there are still hours keeping your finances straight, looking for new assignments, learning new skills, and other distractions that cannot be charged to a client. If you get sick, you are reducing your billable hours. If you take a week, or even a few days, off to ski in Colorado or dive in the Florida Keys, you reduce your available billable time. Realistically, the total of all theses nonbillable items can easily consume half of your

## SALARY VS. BILLABLE RATE, PART 1

| ANNUAL SALARY $40,000 | BILLABLE RATE $50 |
| --- | --- |

EFFECTIVE HOURLY WAGE:

$40,000/2080 HOURS PER YEAR

$19.23 (BEFORE TAXES)

X 2080 FULL-TIME HOURS (40 X 52)

$104,000/YEAR!

...BUT ONLY HALF OF YOUR HOURS ARE BILLABLE.

EFFECTIVE HOURLY WAGE:

$52,000/2080 =

$25 (BEFORE TAXES AND EXPENSES)

figure |5–2|

A billable rate is not the same as an hourly wage, and all the costs of self-employment must be factored into the equation to ensure a fair rate is billed for design work.

time. This reduces your 40-hour workweek to 20 billable hours. The amount you bill your clients must cover the time you cannot bill—this is the unbreakable financial rule of freelancing for a living. With 50% of your time billable, or 1,040 hours to bill in a year, your $50 rate is only going to bring in $52,000. The freelancer, at this point, is still $12,000 ahead of the salary of an equivalent employee.

Of this $52,000 in freelance earnings, there will be some amount that must cover expenses normally absorbed by an employer. This can be as simple and inexpensive as paper for the office printer to the fairly substantial investment in technology and software that most designers must make in the tools of the trade. If this is only a few thousand dollars a year, it still reduces your income. Instead of $12,000 more than a salary, you might be only $9,000 ahead after unbilled expenses, or $49,000 a year.

At this point you must now consider taxes and insurance (see Figure 5–3). As a freelancer, you have no withholdings and are responsible for both the employee and employer portion of federal (and in some cases state) taxes. Even after deductions, this can end up costing you another 25 to 50% of your income. Keep in mind that Self-Employment Tax (Social Security and Medicare Taxes) is 15.3% of your income as a freelancer. So assuming that you are able to deduct a lot of expenses and have keep neat records of everything from business lunches to mileage on your car for work-related trips, your taxes are 30% of your income. That reduces your $52,000 (you pay taxes before expenses, not after) to $36,400. Now reduce that number by unbilled expenses—$3,000 is what we just used, and your yearly take for your $50 an hour billable rate is $33,400. That same amount as an employee would be $16 an hour after taxes, or roughly $20. Working 2,080 hours in a year at $20 an hour, and you get close enough to the $40,000 salary—$41,600—to see that

## SALARY VS. BILLABLE RATE, PART 2

SALARY                         FREELANCE

EFFECTIVE HOURLY: $19.23       $25/HOUR EFFECTIVE
                               ($50/HR, BILLING 50% OF TIME)
$40,000/YEAR
                               $52,000/YEAR

-FEDERAL TAX (25%)             -FEDERAL TAX (25%)
-FICA (7.6%)                   -FICA (15.3%)

($13,040)                      ($20,955)

= $26,960                      = $31,045 ($4085 HIGHER!)

                BUT...   EXPENSES -- HEALTH INSURANCE
                                     COMPUTERS
                                     SOFTWARE
                                     STOCK LIBRARY

                ...NEED TO BE LESS THAN $4085 A YEAR,
                OR IT'S TIME TO RAISE YOUR RATES -
                OR SEND OUT RESUMES.

figure |5–3|

Taxes and insurance can significantly reduce the advantage of billing time over working for an hourly wage or standard salary.

freelancing is not an instant path to riches. Freelance work has its advantages, but as we can see from this example, earnings generally fall in line with the rest of the industry and should not be the primary motivation for staying outside of a firm or in-house department.

Because technology and other big-ticket investments generally are serviceable for a few years, the cost can be spread out over the course of your career. The problem, of course, is that you still have to pay for these things up front. Although there are options to spread the cost out, such as business leasing and other forms of credit, you have to be fairly disciplined to account for spending and return on investment over the long term.

## Freelance Rates

There are many ways to derive a rate for a freelancer, but two are very commonly practiced in the industry. The first is a rule of thumb, or guideline, that allows you to quickly set a rate without a spreadsheet or financial calculator. It is really quite simple. What do you expect you would make, after taxes, per hour, if you were an employee doing the same job? Take that number and

## CALCULATING A RATE: HOURLY X3 RULE

HOURLY RATE:   $25

X3

= $75/HOUR BILLABLE FOR SAME JOB, FREELANCE


ANNUAL
SALARY:        $52,000

HOURS:         2080

$25/HOUR

X3

= $75/HOUR BILLABLE RATE FOR SAME JOB,
FREELANCE

...SO $75/HOUR = ABOUT $52,000/YEAR

figure |5–4|

Although not a scientific way to calculate a rate, multiplying an hourly wage by 3 often gives a good estimate of what the same work would be billed as a freelancer.

multiply it by three (see Figure 5–4). That is your billable rate as a freelancer. This is not advanced numerology or the punch line of a magic trick, it is just a guideline that—like any rule of thumb— generally holds up in practice. If you were to make $16 an hour, your billable rate would be $48 an hour. If you were making $25 an hour, your billable rate would be $75 an hour. A firm principal or other high-level strategic creative person who is in the low six figures might be making, after taxes, the equivalent of $50 an hour over the course of a year. This level of work on a freelance basis or as part of a small boutique consultancy might command $150 or more an hour.

At the other end of the spectrum, you might be willing to get experience in the field as an employee making $12 an hour. A freelance rate of $36 would ensure you could cover your taxes and expenses. The rule of thumb that a billable rate is triple an hourly wage works assuming you treat your freelance work as a serious business endeavor. The trap many designers starting out make is that they want to freelance and, for fear of losing out on work, shortchange themselves. Do not think you are alone if you thought you could pocket freelance income without paying taxes or use software that is not licensed to you (or not licensed for professional use). This sort of think- ing creates the idea that a $20 an hour freelance assignment is paying more than a $14 an hour job. Although this is technically true, the client paying you the low rate and looking the other way at issues such as taxes is generally not on the hook if there is a problem. As a freelance designer, it is your responsibility to protect your own interests, pay your own taxes, and be accountable for your own work. A good client understands that design is a valuable professional service and will not try to price you into a difficult situation, such as an audit, that could haunt you later.

## CALCULATING A RATE: EXPENSES + INCOME/HOURS

### ESTIMATED EXPENSES:

OFFICE
COMPUTER
SOFTWARE
HEALTH INSURANCE          $25,000
BUSINESS INSURANCE
STOCK LIBRARY

### ESTIMATED REQUIRED INCOME          $50,000

+ TAXES (FEDERAL)          + $10,000
+ TAXES (LOCAL AND STATE)  + $5,000     $22,500
+ TAXES (FICA - 15.3%)     + $7,500

### TOTAL:                             $97,500

### HOURS BILLABLE:

20 HOURS/WEEK          X 50 WEEKS = 1000

RATE = $97.50/HOUR

figure |5–5|

A more formal way to set an hourly rate uses available hours to bill clients per year and expected expenses to arrive at annual income.

Although the triple rule does hold up, the more formal approach to setting a rate is also useful to employ. It takes a bit of math, but is fairly straightforward. Add up your expenses, including your own salary you would reasonably expect to earn. Determine the number of hours in a year you plan to bill. Divide these two numbers. For example, if your required income and expenses add up to $100,000 in a year and you reasonably expect to bill 1,000 hours (20 hours a week for 50 weeks with 2 weeks per year off), your billable rate would be 100,000 divided by 1,000, or $100 an hour (see Figure 5–5).

This time-honored formula does, however, have a serious flaw. What if two designers of equal educational backgrounds, talent, and experience have wildly different expenses? In an increasingly global business climate, what is a "reasonable salary" if your client is in Nebraska and you work from New York? What if the opposite is true, and you live in an area with a low cost of living and your clients work from Class A office space in the world's most expensive cities? The amount of hours you may have available is fairly set, but your expenses could be much higher or much lower than other designers.

The question of expenses is a difficult one and can be handled different ways when you set your billable rates. First, make sure you understand the going rates for your type of work. The major design organizations, such as AIGA and The Graphic Artists Guild, publish this data each year, and it is very important that you have an idea of what clients are paying. If your personal billable rate is calculated to be higher than the going rate for your work, you have two options. You can lower the rate to suit the market and expect that your higher expenses—such as an apartment in a large urban area—avails you to more opportunity and is worth the increased expense. The other approach is to stick to your rate and take less work. If you are confident in the service you provide and see your rate as a reflection of your own quality, you may be better off to take fewer clients than compete on price with designers around the world.

If your personal rate is less than the market rate, you have a similar decision to make. You could use the surplus to save for the future or build your business, or you could cut your rate to try to earn more work. In general, if your work is high quality you are better off not to severely discount yourself. One change in life—the purchase of a home, your first child, going back to school to earn an MFA—and your low rate might not work for you any longer. The problem at that point is that you have built your client base on an unsustainably low billable rate, and now have to justify market rates that you should have been earning already.

The market will usually dictate billable rates, or at least the starting point in negotiations. If you do illustration and your clients are willing to pay up to $35 an hour, your calculations might lead you to a rate that is too high to get the work.

Again, speed and efficiency is vitally important (see Figure 5–6). If you need to make $60 an hour but your client is only willing to pay $35 an hour, you could still be the right illustrator if you deliver twice as fast as other artists they are considering. The client might scoff at $60 per hour, but had planned on an illustrator billing $35 an hour for 10 hours to complete an assignment. With a budget of $350, you could still do the assignment if you could complete the work in half the allotted time, or 5 hours. Your total invoice to the client is still within their $350 budget, but they paid you $70 per hour for 5 hours instead of $35 for 10 hours. Most clients are ultimately concerned about cost, not just your rate, so it is important to talk with your prospects about the overall budget of an assignment. You may find that you work fast enough to satisfy their needs, but are still able to make a decent rate on the work.

Firm: LogoWorks

Client: The Red Rockets, a little league baseball team.

## SPEED: QUICK WORK IN A SPECIALTY CAN MAKE LOW BUDGET JOBS PROFITABLE

CLIENT OFFERS
$350, FIXED PRICE

ESTIMATES 10 HOUR JOB
AT $35/HOUR

DESIGNER NEEDS $50/HOUR

WORKS FAST ON SPECIFIC
TYPE OF PRODUCT

COMPLETS JOB IN 5 HOURS

CLIENT PAYS $350 ⟶ DESIGNER EARNS $350/5
= $70/HOUR

figure |5–6|

The client's budget is only one-half of the equation to determine a profitable project. Equally important is how long the work will take you to complete.

### How do you bill seconds?

Design is ultimately problem solving, and some solutions do take time to think through and consider. But how do you bill hourly when an idea pops into your head in an instant? This is one of the problems of using hourly rates, and why strategic creative work can be harder to quantify than lower-level tasks such as production and layout. If you are creating an annual report in Adobe InDesign and work at relatively the same speed of your peers, hourly billing can work well for you and your client. But after hours of research and meetings and competitive analysis, how much time does it take to dream up the core idea for a global marketing campaign or new product? Maybe 10 minutes or 10 months, but the answer is a moot point. In either case, the client and the creative staff are not really doing work suitable for hourly rates. This sort of high-level creative often works better with fixed cost or fee-based arrangements. Having said that, many design professionals still track their time to projects so the firm can refine their processes and pricing based on how their staff works. Although it may not reflect in the invoice of any specific project, as the number of hours generally does not alter a fixed fee project, the firm will still want to know how much time the staff spends on each account. This information is important to create a good understanding of the capacity of the firm and in knowing if any one account is taking too much staff time for the fee to justify long term.

# Fixed Cost

For purposes of budgeting a project, tracking hours and affixing billable rates can leave a client with a moving target, a nebulous projection that is not solid enough to count on for months, or even years, of work. Although they may have a reasonable certainty that accurate accounts of hours spent on a project will be invoiced, an open-ended agreement of a certain amount per hour with a new designer can sometimes be viewed as a blank check to a business owner or manager. For this reason, the business may be more comfortable with assigning a fixed amount to a project or to each deliverable within a project. Fixed cost can also be easier for the designer to manage, as well. Instead of remembering to start or stop your watch (or software) every time the phone rings to track billable time, the designer can count on a certain amount over the course of a project. Fixed cost projects do mean, however, the designer must calculate their expected time expenditure and determine whether the project is within a target hourly rate. Fixed cost projects can be great opportunities to earn a good billable rate for your time, but can also be terrifying to a freelancer (see Figure 5–7). If you worked quickly and get the work done and signed off, the budget

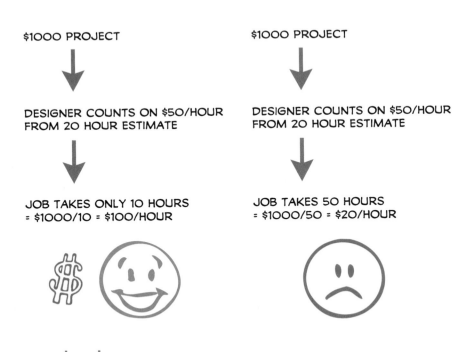

## FIXED COST: RISK AND OPPORTUNITY

$1000 PROJECT

DESIGNER COUNTS ON $50/HOUR FROM 20 HOUR ESTIMATE

JOB TAKES ONLY 10 HOURS = $1000/10 = $100/HOUR

$1000 PROJECT

DESIGNER COUNTS ON $50/HOUR FROM 20 HOUR ESTIMATE

JOB TAKES 50 HOURS = $1000/50 = $20/HOUR

figure |5–7|

A fixed cost project that can cause you to work for less than your billable rate or be an opportunity to earn more per hour than you would otherwise charge.

may prove to be much more than you would have been able to charge hourly. Many freelancers make a living at this type of project, especially when they are able to reuse elements or code or even layouts from previous work to save even more time. The flip side, and the risk of taking fixed cost projects, is that the project could take considerably more time than you expected.

As an example, a client might offer $1,000 as a fixed cost for a small project. If your target billable rate is $50, you must determine whether this project will take 20 or fewer hours to complete. In one scenario, everything goes perfectly and you complete the job in 8 hours. Your effective billable rate is now $1,000 divided by 8, or $125 an hour. However, if you run into problems completing the work, the same project could take you 28 hours to complete. Your effective billable rate is now $1,000 divided by 28, or only $35.71 per hour.

As you can see, working efficiently is important even when the client does not know your rate and hours, and the cost of the job is fixed. Many designers run into serious time management issues before they learn the importance it plays in making a living as a freelancer. A designer with fine art training might sweat every detail of a deliverable, far beyond the client's expectations, but in doing so pushes the effective billable rate from $75 an hour to $7.50 an hour. The balance between maintaining quality and working in a time efficient manner is one of the most critical things to learn about working in the creative professions. Striking this balance on every single project is almost impossible, of course, so effective designers learn how to budget their time across multiple projects. A project that you thought would take 10 hours to complete, for example, but instead took 6 gives you 4 hours the client already paid for that might help offset another project that took longer than you expected. This is why experienced designers complain to each other about projects that overrun expected time but choose carefully when to voice the same discontent to a client. A good client who does not intentionally pay less than a fair rate is usually worth keeping, so if one project takes too long to complete, another may soon follow that will more than make up the difference (see Figure 5–8).

Another consideration when choosing fixed cost work is that new clients and completely new projects always take longer than a familiar client asking for something they routinely need. This is another area that is not an exact science, but most designers and even larger firms expect the work performed for a client not to be fully profitable until a second, third, or even fourth engagement. It only makes sense that the first time you work with a client you will need to do more research and spend more time working with them to understand their needs than the second project, when you will already have a good grasp on what they expect and how their market is structured. With this in mind, your first project might leave off some of the time you spend getting ready for the work with the intent of using the same price on future work to make up the difference. Although this can be a smart approach if managed carefully, it can also bury new designers in a constant cycle of hoping the next project is the one that earns a fair wage. Always start with your billable rate in mind, and do not lead the discussion with a significant discount unless you have a solid expectation this client will be sending you more work soon. Another way to handle this is to charge your full rate on the initial project but offer attractive discounts to the client for repeat business.

Within fixed cost, there is also fixed fee arrangements. This is generally used for clients that need a certain amount of work each month or quarter and want to budget the amount a creative firm charges them into their longer-term plans. For example, a client that needs at least $5,000 in work each month, but sometimes slightly more or less, might agree to a fixed fee of this amount

# FIXED COST: MULTIPLE PROJECTS

| | | | |
|---|---|---|---|
| PROJECT 1: | $1000 | ESTIMATED: 20 HOURS | ACTUAL: 30 HOURS |
| | | | EARNED: $1000/30 = $33.33   UNDER ▬ |

| | | | |
|---|---|---|---|
| PROJECT 2: | $5000 | ESTIMATED: 100 HOURS | ACTUAL: 90 HOURS |
| | | | EARNED: $5000/90 = $55.56   OVER ╋ |

| | | | |
|---|---|---|---|
| PROJECT 3: | $2000 | ESTIMATED: 40 HOURS | ACTUAL: 45 HOURS |
| | | | EARNED: $2000/45 = $44.44   UNDER ▬ |

| | | | |
|---|---|---|---|
| PROJECT 4: | $3000 | ESTIMATED: 60 HOURS | ACTUAL: 50 HOURS |
| | | | EARNED: $3000/50 = $60.00   OVER ╋ |

| TOTAL FROM CLIENT: | EXPECTED RATE: | ACTUAL RATE: |
|---|---|---|
| $11,000 | $50/HOUR | 215 HOURS |
| | | $11,000/215 ACTUAL HOURS |
| | | = $51.16/HOUR |

RESULT: KEEP CLIENT, EVEN THOUGH HALF THE PROJECTS DON'T PAYREQUIRED RATE!
THE LONGER, HIGH-DOLLAR PROJECTS COVER THE DIFFERENCE.

figure |5–8|

Even if single project takes too much time and is a loss, a designer can usually make his or her required rate over the course of several fixed cost projects.

in exchange for a break on the hourly rate or the guaranteed delivery of a certain amount of work. This arrangement works well for firms with established client relationships, especially in advertising, but is less common for freelancers. Fixed fee clients offer the chance to really work on the strategic side of the business, as there is less emphasis on any one deliverable than there is on the overall direction of the client's brand (see Figure 5–9).

It is important to consider that even in a fixed fee situation, there is no escaping the importance of time management for a creative firm. The same basic principle of charging a rate per hour multiplied by the number of hours applies to a fixed fee client. The difference lies in presentation to the client. While firms vary in their disclosure to clients of actual hours, this time must still be tracked internally. This allows the management of the firm to properly assess the profitability of the client relationship.

figure |5–9|

Image courtesy of Fine Design Group.

## Per Diem

Another way to calculate a rate for professional services is called per diem, or day rate. This might be offered to a designer to join a project for a few days instead of a negotiated rate per hour. The basis for a per diem rate is still hours, but allows the designer to block out the entire day for the client.

This is especially useful for work that requires the designer to be on-site. For example, an art director based in Minnesota who needs to be present at a photo shoot in New York might require the client to pay per diem rather than hourly because it is unreasonable to expect any hours during the trip will be free for other clients. The same job locally might be billed hourly, as it may only take part of a business day to complete.

## Opportunity Costs

It might seem that a client willing to pay a monthly fee to keep an ongoing relationship with a design firm would be a great benefit. While this can be true, the same litmus test must be applied to each client—How much time is being spent for a given amount of money? Over the course of several months, even fixed fee clients must prove to be profitable for a design firm to keep the relationship. It is an easy trap to fall into that a client offering $1,000 per month must, by default, be a relationship worth maintaining. However, if the client is requiring work of 20, 40, or 100 hours each month, the effective rate of the work falls to $50 per hour, $25 an hour, or $10 an hour respectively. Many fixed fee clients understand that their base fee only covers a certain amount of work and will expect additional charges as reasonable. If this is not the understanding of both parties though, the client may object and expect increasing amounts of work without additional compensation. As hard as it is to release a paying customer, the relationship with a client that does not pay your required billable rate must be terminated for the business to survive.

The reason for terminating such a relationship is called opportunity cost (see Figure 5–10). As discussed earlier, each designer and firm have a limited number of hours available to bill clients. If these hours are spent on a client paying below your target billable rate, the work is costing you in two ways. The first is that you are making less per hour than you require. The second, more hidden cost is losing the opportunity to use that time in a more effective way, such as working for a client who will pay your billable rate. This is not to say you should wildly overreact the first time your client needs more hours than you budgeted. But opportunity cost does suggest that you must only keep clients who, over time, allow you to earn a living and make a profit for your firm. There are some situations beyond financial calculation that suggest keeping a client, such as nonprofits or high-profile work in an industry you want to market your services, that does not meet this requirement but overall your client base must support your billable rate.

### OPPORTUNITY COST

|  | MONTH 1 | MONTH 2 | MONTH 3 |
|---|---|---|---|
| CLIENT PAYING $25/HOUR | NEEDS 15 HOURS PER WEEK | NEEDS 15 HOURS PER WEEK | NEEDS 15 HOURS PER WEEK |
| DESIGNER REQUIRES $50/HOUR TO COVER EXPENSES | 15 HOURS TAKEN AT $25/HOUR | 15 HOURS TAKEN AT $25/HOUR | NEW CLIENT PAYS $50/HOUR |
| 40 HOURS PER WEEK AVAILABLE | 25 HOURS FREE AT $50/HOUR | 25 HOURS FREE AT $50/HOUR | NEEDS 40 HOURS PER WEEK |

...DESIGNER MUST RELEASE UNDERPAYING CLIENT. NOT ENOUGH HOURS TO GO AROUND!

figure |5–10|  A client who pays each month is hard to let go, but there is an opportunity cost to doing work that does not meet your minimum billable rate over the course of several projects.

Joie de Vivre Hotels

Creative Director: Kenn Fine

Designer: Melissa Chan

Developers: Tsilli Pines, Scott Brisko, Jason Fine, Mathias Baske

Project Director: Lori Dunkin

Courtesy of Fine Design Group

In a travel situation, the per diem may also include expenses such as the cost of a hotel room and some amount to cover meals. In a city that requires driving, such as Los Angeles, the cost of a rental car and fuel may also be factored into the per diem. This allows the client to pay a rate per day and not have to pay for your time and expenses in separate, detailed invoices. Per diem for travel also allows the designer to decide for themselves how to live while on the project without explanation of specific expenses. This allows one designer to apply their per diem toward a luxury hotel but fast food dinners, whereas another might choose to stay in a modest hotel room but eat (or drink) well after a full day of meetings with a client.

Per diem is very common among creative services that work with designers, such as copywriting and photography. A copywriter, for example, may bill hourly or per project also, but will often be closely involved in the project and be expected at meetings and other tasks that are hard to quantify exactly as billable. Because a copywriter works in text and does not require specialized software, he or she could spend time with a client away from their desk, such as a business lunch, and be actively creating. Billed hourly, this type of collaboration could be debatable as to when the copywriter is working on the project, so per diem allocates a full workday to the project with no confusion or negotiation required.

## Time and Materials

The most direct way to bill a project is, of course, by time and materials used. As the phrase implies, the client is obliged to pay for expenses incurred during the production of their work. This method is not too common among designers, but is with certain creative services in the industry. For example, a photographer might negotiate a rate that includes time and materials so that everything, even the cost of fuel in their car and the tolls on the freeway, is billed to the client for a custom photo shoot. This was an important distinction when professional photographers had to use expensive film and chemicals to do their work, but there are still other materials that require the client to pay more than a standard labor rate. A photographer may still incur expenses to set up a shoot that are outside of the norm, and these may be billed to the client.

In general, any creative project that requires extensive investment that is not in the generally expected realm of what a design firm should own—such as their computers, design software, and printers—may be billed as time and materials. The important consideration as a designer is that expenses incurred to work for a client do not consume your profits or standard hourly rate. Any project that has outside expenses may require a freelancer to seek compensation for such items, and it is important to clearly spell out these charges before they are incurred. An hourly or per diem rate is usually assumed to include expenses unless the designer states otherwise, so it is best to be up front about costs you feel are specific to the project and allow the client to budget for them.

This method is very comprehensive, and can be attractive to designers who are starting out and simply do not have the financial resources to absorb any project expenses, but time and materials billing is not really a preferred way to do business. Time and materials requires even more tracking than billing hourly, and the additional paperwork and record keeping takes away from the profit of the job. Of course, billing a client for materials often means extensive negotiation of charges and a level of transparency that is uncomfortable. An experienced designer will often be able to make an educated guess about the expenses the project will incur and factor that into a simpler billing method, such as fixed cost or a standard hourly rate.

Firm: Damashek Consulting

Client: Bacardi Global Brands

Project Description: Bacardi Global Brands partnered with Damashek Consulting to redesign the Bombay Sapphire Web site to create a high-impact, multimedia site experience befitting the super premium spirit.

---

### Q&A Ask the Pros:
### Overcoming Adversity, Audelino Moreno, TBD Advertising

*Q: What are some of the significant differences between school and professional work?*
A: One of the biggest things is that you really have to live with frustrations everyday, like having an idea you really liked rejected by the client. You have to go back to the drawing board and think again and see it as an opportunity. You cannot get frustrated and think "I will just give the client what they want" and you have to discipline yourself to say "okay, it was rejected, but let me see if I can do something even better."

---

# PROJECT SCOPE

With a good understanding of what to charge, the other half of the proposal equation is the size of the project. This is often referred to as scope. Freelancers and firms use many different proposal formats, some defining scope very precisely item by item and others using more general terms. This depends largely on the type of work and the relationship with the client. Many of the firms interviewed for this book mentioned using a more concise, easy-to-read project definition (and proposal, overall) than in years past. This trend, while not verified across the industry, is likely a natural result of business decision makers having more information to consume and more time pressure than ever before. A long, wandering proposal that does not get to the key points—what are they buying, when will they have it, and what does it cost—is less likely to succeed in today's business environment. On the flip side, a project scope defines your product and can expose you or your firm to legal entanglements if you do not carefully spell out the boundaries of the project.

If your product is your own time, as it may be for freelance work, the project scope should clearly define how much time you are committing to the project. It should also include the time frame in which these hours are applied—normal business hours in your time zone during the workweek, for example. Finally, you do not want to leave yourself open to owing a previous client more of your time after you thought the project was over. The scope should also limit how long your services are available—40 hours within the next 30 days, for example—so that you do not have too many overlapping requests for your time.

## Deliverables

The proposal must spell out what the client can expect from the project. The deliverables list is often how this is put in writing and may differ slightly from the actual goal of the project. For example, the project might be to redesign the identity of the client. An example of a deliverable would be five logo concepts in PDF format. Although the final logo might be delivered in several different variations (CMYK, RGB, grayscale, word marks, regional differences, animated) and file formats (EPS, PDF, JPEG, GIF), this work would be a separate deliverable. There are a few reasons for drawing the distinction between the first and the second set of logos in a deliverable section of a proposal.

The first reason is to protect you. You do not want any confusion over deliverables. Your client should have a clear understanding of what you are going to provide, and this should be in writing. If you expect to deliver a final logo in one format suitable for black and white newsprint and the client is expecting something they can immediately use as an animated interstitial ad or online video, the deliverables list should solve this disagreement.

The second reason why a designer must always spell out deliverables is because of the unpredictable nature of business. A project can be cancelled or materially changed at any time for a variety of reasons that are outside of the designer's control, including management turnover or changes to budgets or competitive offerings. A deliverables list puts in writing the pieces of the project, not just the final output, and allows both the designer and the client to see where the project stands at any point.

If your deliverable list is too short or too general—a new website, for example—the components of the project that must be created along the way are not included in the contract. This creates an all or nothing discussion of whether the project is complete, instead of a more reasonable assessment of what was delivered and what remains before the complete site is signed off.

Deliverables also allow your proposal to assign costs to steps within the project, not just the final solution. This is important for many clients that might not understand how a creative project works or how costs evolve from all the hours applied to the work. This is also important if the project does end up cancelled or delayed, as the costs of each item are spelled out. Again, if there is no deliverables list, the client has the ability—perhaps legally more than ethically—to assign the project no value as the end product was not completed. To protect yourself from this situation, make sure each deliverable, or at least small group of deliverables, have value assigned.

> ### A la Carte Creative?
>
> A deliverables list should not mean that your solution is a loose collection of parts that can be ordered like adding French fries to a fast food meal. Although you want to ensure each element of your proposal has an assigned value, be careful to explain in your proposal that your solution cannot be purchased by line item. For small clients especially, the temptation will be to shortchange the project at the end and find cheaper labor once the core solution is complete. This can severely cut into your profit on a project, because the number of hours you spent on earlier milestones might have been more than you projected. You can make up for this by adding what is known as a kill fee. Kill fees are more common among writers, and while you might use less harsh terminology ("project cancellation charge" perhaps) there should be some contractual basis for you to ask for money to offset your loss. Another approach that is fairly common among designers is to set the payments on the project in line with major deliverables. In this manner, you can ensure that if a client cancels before the end of the project (to avoid the last payments) you are not obligated to deliver the core result of the project.

## Assumptions

Assumptions, in terms of a proposal, are just stated declarations of items that might affect the outcome of a project. For example, if you are designing a new Internet site for a client, an assumption might be that the client will provide the server (or hosting account) that meets the particular requirements of your project and gives you proper access to upload your files. By stating this, you are putting on paper things you expect are true about the project, but may not be. If your assumptions are found to be false, such as the client expecting you to provide your own server for the new website, the assumptions page of the contract can be referenced to protect you from additional expense and time. Because technology changes so quickly and can so greatly affect design projects, this is the most common area to use assumptions.

Print projects can also use assumptions regarding the printer, paper used, or other specifics. Again, the focus is to make sure variances in the project do not cost you unbilled hours or cash. Other assumptions might be the desired use of the project, such as specifying to an international client that all copywriting will be in English or the number of franchise locations that will use the creative output of the project. Although it may not be immediately obvious that these assumptions are even relevant, if they help to define the project and avoid later debate they are probably worth writing out. If you frequently work with similar clients, you will find your assumptions page will not need much editing from project to project and can just be inserted into each proposal.

# PROJECT MANAGEMENT

With the proposal signed by the client, the focus turns to delivering the work. For many firms this will take the form of a meeting between all the members of both the firm and the client. The project does not start with art, and the quality of artwork in the project is not the most critical factor in the success of the engagement. Effective project management is designed to enable communication and problem solving, and this is usually a time consuming back and forth of ideas even before a sketchbook is used to start laying out concepts. Clients can be fickle, and many feel it is their right to change their minds or push the creative team in different directions until they are satisfied with the outcome of the project.

Many primary contacts on design projects, especially for larger clients, are not designers and have no design training. The expertise they may have in navigating the design process is often from previous work with other firms, so, in effect, your project is part of their learning process. Good project managers understand how to balance this situation, as delicate egos of senior executives (and perhaps find a tactful way to say, "If you would let us, our team can be creative without your input") and looming deadlines compete for attention. The project management concepts we discuss here is just a part of the larger picture of seeing a project through to completion. Every designer uses, or should use, some form of documentation of project progress, be able to show interdependencies between work steps, and get change orders signed when the project veers off course.

## The Paper Trail

E-mail may not be actual paper, but some form of written communication is vital at all stages of a project. Although trust between client and design firm is important, the demands of modern business dictate that mistakes happen, conversations are forgotten, and what is agreed in meetings is not always heard the same way by all involved. The multitasking, fast-paced world of design also further exacerbates the "telephone game" problem—when a story (or any detail of the project) is told from one person to the next, the story changes. By the time a third or fourth person is involved in the discussion, the entire context of what was said may be lost. Therefore, while many designers do not like the bureaucracy of documenting everything in a project, the paper trail is very important when any business discussion takes place.

Another reason project management is largely a written process is the changes to personnel a company may undergo during an engagement. If designers or other staff move on to another employer in the middle of project, they may leave with knowledge of important decisions or client approvals that were not forwarded on to others on your team. This must be retrievable information, as most corporate e-mail systems are, and can save days of backtracking and piecing together notes from meetings and client phone calls. As much as it seems mundane, the habit of typing up a quick e-mail to confirm what was said—in meetings or on the phone—between client and designer is a good practice to observe.

A last reason for the documentation of each phase of the project is that it is commercial work. When money changes hands in a business transaction, there is always the possibility of legal issues arising. It is best to protect yourself at each step of a project by putting it in writing. This is even more critical when rights issues are involved, such as licensing illustration or photography. While a phone call from a trusted client to say you can use an image might seem good enough to continue working towards a deadline, the lack of any documentation to approve the image could leave you, or your firm, culpable if the rights to the image were not purchased for such use. This lack of documentation could end up costing thousands of dollars if the work is on a major ad campaign, for example.

# Dependencies

One of the more common information graphics used in project management is a Gantt chart. The Gantt chart represents time on the horizontal axis, and each work step is then drawn on the chart to show how long it is expected to take. At a glance, everyone on a project team can see on a Gantt chart the approaching deadlines and next steps of the project (see Figure 5–11).

Gantt charts are frequently used because they can show the relationship between different steps in a project. When one step in a project must be completed for another to continue, it is known as a dependency. Dependencies are important to understand for project managers and other members of the design team, because they show what is called the critical path. In each project, there are steps that must be done in order and be completed on time for the project to proceed on schedule. These steps, taken together, follow from the project launch to final signoff by the client. This is known as the critical path, tracing the steps that must occur in order, on time.

Other steps in a project may create or rely on dependencies, but may be ancillary to the project. These are not on the critical path, and resources may be diverted from them if a deadline is approaching that may not be met. Other steps in the project may not have dependencies and may fit into the schedule as resources are available.

**GANTT CHART**

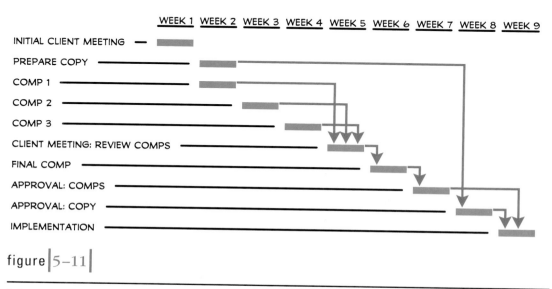

figure 5–11

A Gantt chart is one way to keep track of how one step of a project depends on the successful completion of another.

For example, an annual report project might include a step to conduct an outdoor photo shoot of the corporate campus. Getting these images to the client for approval would depend on the photo shoot occurring on time. This is a dependency. The approved images being used in a layout comp would then have a dependency on the previous step of client approval.

Now assume in our example that it rains on the corporate campus for a period of two days. Without charting dependencies, it would be easy to assume that this shoot is simply delayed and the project itself is on track for timely completion. However, because this photo shoot has dependent steps, all of these are now delayed also. An effective project manager must account for this in allocating resources and, most important, communicating with the client that the rain altered the critical path to the project.

Common tools like Microsoft Project allow firms to easily create Gantt charts, and there are other charts that also allow for effective project management. The key to understand is the dependencies of work within the team, and between the client and the team, to a successful project. The larger the project scale, the more this becomes critical, as multiyear engagements such as corporate rebranding can have hundreds of steps and many dependencies to watch over. These steps require frequent communication and documentation not to get badly off schedule, wasting time and misappropriating what would otherwise be billable time of designers, art directors, copywriters, and other creative professionals.

## Change Orders

Despite the best intentions, very few proposals match the end result of a project exactly. As the project develops, the client may want more than the original proposal—and the original cost—covered. There may be substantial changes as collaboration sparks new ideas. Or the client may reveal they have more work that needs to be done once they like the firm they have hired. Whatever the reason, if the project changes, the firm must document the change and the client must sign some agreement that states they did in fact request the change. This is known as a change order. Change orders can save time and money in several ways.

First, a change order forces a client to reconsider whether they do want additional work done. Many requests by clients are not thought out and, when put in writing, will have less appeal. The change order acts as a last chance to waive off the new direction and continue the present course of the project. This is again something a skillful project manager must handle with tact. A client can be put off by a change order if there is any appearance of apprehension on the part of the designer or design firm. Managing the client relationship effectively includes presenting change orders in a manner that shows appreciation for the additional work and not resistance to change.

Second, the change order allows the design firm the chance to attach a price to the additional work. This is an area that many designers, especially inexperienced freelancers, lose an opportunity to earn additional income. A serious buyer of creative work understands that if they ask for more work than what was agreed they must pay additional hours or some other amount. However, many artists do not want to break the flow of the project or get anxious about raising the price of their work and execute change orders with no additional cost. This critical error can reduce the effective billable rate of a project severely. Taking on additional work without properly accounting for it often creates loathing and distrust on the part of the designer—a feeling of being taken advantage of by the client. This situation can lead the designer to become jaded about the work and the industry as a whole. Before that happens, the proper course is to require additional payment for additional services. This leads to a more professional relationship that does not end up a lopsided, constant stream of requests for free work.

Finally, the change order allows the firm to adequately adjust all related project schedules. As discussed in the section on Dependencies, each step in the process may cause delays in additional steps. If the client requires new or modified work during the course of the project, the firm must look at how this will affect the time frame of the project. Depending on the current workload and capacity of the firm, other clients could be affected as well. It is up to the management of the firm to account for and document these issues before agreeing to the changes.

- Fine art and commercial art is not the same thing and must be treated differently—from representation to pricing to legal issues—but you can have a career in both if you treat them as different pursuits.
- Even if you or your firm uses fixed fees or project-based pricing, tracking your time is the only way to reliably know whether the work is profitable.
- Freelancers must remember that a large portion of their yearly schedule will be spent on tasks they cannot bill clients for, such as self-promotion, administrative tasks, and learning new skills.
- A fixed cost project can be opportunity to earn more per hour than you could normally charge, but can also average out poorly if the project takes longer than expected.
- Longer-term client relationships allow designers to average time across multiple fixed cost projects to ensure a fair billable rate.
- Scope is the size and breadth of the project: the amount of work that will be done.
- What the client is buying, when the project will be delivered, and what it costs are the key points and minimum questions to answer in the proposal.
- A deliverables list puts in writing the pieces of the project, not just the final output, and allows both the designer and the client to see where the project stands at any point.
- Project management is largely a written process because of staff turnover—resignations, firing and hiring staff, and reassigning project resources.

**THE BOTTOM LINE**

# LEGAL ISSUES

# introduction

There are several major legal areas that a designer must become familiar with to successfully navigate the business world. The most important of these is intellectual property. The ownership and right to exclusively earn income from creative work is legally protected and transferred by copyright, trademark, and patent laws. In this chapter, we look at each of these areas in depth, and also look at common work arrangements and the effect these have on your rights and employment.

# objectives

The core legal issues of intellectual property as they relate to the design profession.

How copyright is assigned and registered.

How your work agreement determines whether you, your employer, or your client actually own your design work.

The concept of fair use, and when you can legally use copyrighted material.

How a trademark differs from a copyright, and when each is appropriate.

What nondisclosure and noncompete agreements are and when it is reasonable for a client or employer to request them of you.

What spec work is and why you should avoid it.

# INTELLECTUAL PROPERTY

The career, income, and reputation of a designer are largely based on bringing intangible ideas to life. Unlike other industries, in which the delivered product is often one you can hold in your hand, design deals in ethereal qualities. Everyone in America knows Coca-Cola or Starbucks or Google, but the financial value of these firms is largely in the recognition and meaning of their brands and the collective knowledge of their processes (see Figure 6–1). This value makes the laws that govern and protect what is created in the mind—*intellectual property*—especially important. Intellectual property is not a law, per se, but a group of laws and legal concepts that deal with who owns and has right to profit from new creations—art, inventions, this book, photographs—and for how long.

Intellectual property laws also set the legality of how works can be used, traded, and transferred. It is intellectual property laws that outlined the legality of watching a movie you purchased and the illegality of watching an exact digital copy of the same movie that was not authorized by the studio. In this section, we explore the key concepts a designer must understand about intellectual property to avoid legal entanglements and protect their own work. Although design deliverables often appear on tangible media, from letterhead to the hood of a race car, the work is that of ideas, concepts, color, shape, and form; design creates more intellectual property than real property and it is this area that designers must be most familiar with to understand the value they create and how that value is protected legally.

## INTELLECTUAL PROPERTY IN DAILY LIFE

TECHNOLOGY:

SOFTWARE PATENTS
HARDWARE PATENTS
END USER LICENSING
TRADEMARKS

MUSIC:

COPYRIGHTED SONGS, LYRICS, SHEET MUSIC
INSTRUMENT PATENTS
TRADEMARKS FOR BANDS, LABELS
LICENSED DISTRIBUTION

AUTOMOTIVE:

ENGINEERING PATENTS
MANUFACTURING PATENTS
TRADEMARKS

FILM:

COPYRIGHTED SCREENPLAYS
FINISHED FILMS
PATENTED EFFECTS
LICENSED DISTRIBUTION

FOOD

TRADEMARKS:
TRADE SECRETS
PATENTED GROWING METHODS
PATENTED COOKING/DELIVERY METHODS

figure |6–1|

Intellectual property laws are a major part of many industries and affect many areas of modern life.

# Copyright

When you create an original work as an artist, musician, photographer, or inventor, you are granted *copyright* to it. Copyright laws protect most work generally thought of as art along with books and other creative expression. Music, video, and even software are now also within the domain of copyright. However, your next great idea cannot—in and of itself—be copyrighted. Concepts and ideas cannot be protected as original work; just as very broad storylines (a movie about a criminal that gets caught by a detective) are not specific enough to copyright. Other very general use items, such as the color brown, cannot be copyrighted; however, use of brown in a consistent way in the act of commerce may be legally protected as part of a *trademark*. An international shipping company using brown on uniforms and trucks, for example, may be violating the UPS trademark.

Copyright laws are intended to give the creator of a work an exclusive right to take advantage of their creation. The basic concept, as it evolved from seventeenth-century English royalty and is spelled out in Article 1 of the U.S. Constitution, is that authors and inventors should be granted a period of time to exclusively deal in their work to encourage progress and the advancement of society, culture, science, and the arts. Although abuses of copyright laws and the legal wrangling of Fortune 500 firms may seem only slightly related to this goal, as a designer it is still important to realize the laws are there for this purpose and should be used to your advantage (see Figure 6–2).

The first area copyright protects is the reproduction of the work. If you create an illustration or shoot a photograph, your copyright allows you to reproduce the work. Now that design is a largely digital process, this capability includes files that can easily be duplicated around the world in seconds and becomes very difficult to control or track. However, the copyright holder is technically the only one afforded the right to duplicate and sell the work. It is this area of copyright

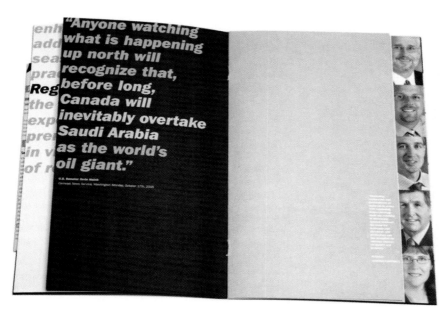

figure|6–2|

Client: Burnet, Duckworth & Palmer LLP (or BD&P), a Calgary-based law firm that Design by Sasges Inc.

that is the centerpiece of thousands of lawsuits in the music business, as duplicated digital audio tracks quickly find their way to users that are not licensed to retain copies of the files.

Another right granted to the creator of a work is adaptation. If you create, and therefore hold copyright to, a comic book and a film studio wants to make it into a screenplay, they would need your permission to do so. In most cases, the studio would compensate you for this use of your intellectual property.

As a copyright holder, you are allowed to modify the work. If you walk into a museum with a spray can and deface another artist's painting, you would be violating their copyright. You would legally be allowed to do so to your own painting. One area that is a more blurred line in the law is how much you can modify a copyrighted work without infringement. It is common for designers to assure firm principals and clients that their modifications of existing work—using a program like Adobe Photoshop to edit a copyrighted photo beyond recognition, for example—are legal and create an entirely new work. This is often not the case, as the line between inspiration and infringement is easy to cross with modern design technology.

Along the same lines, the copyright holder is entitled to make *derivative works* of their original (see Figure 6–3). A work derived from copyrighted work might be a sequel to a film or a limited edition poster series based on an original illustration. The concept of derivative works is important in the design business because most corporate communication is intended for several different media. Websites based on brochures, video based on magazine ads, ad jingles based on hit music, illustration created from photographs—all could be derivative works and therefore may require the permission of the original copyright holder.

## DERIVATIVE WORKS

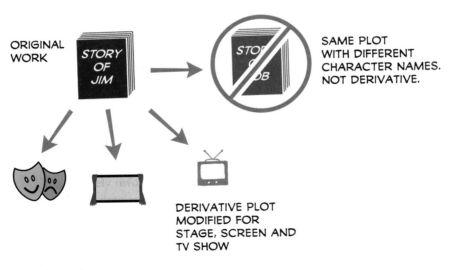

ORIGINAL WORK

STORY OF JIM

SAME PLOT WITH DIFFERENT CHARACTER NAMES. NOT DERIVATIVE.

DERIVATIVE PLOT MODIFIED FOR STAGE, SCREEN AND TV SHOW

figure |6–3|

Many motion pictures are based on, or derived from, plot and characters that originally appear in book form. Similarly, a novel that uses plot, characters, or situations based on a movie could be a derivative work.

As an artist or creator, you own the copyright at the point your new creative work is completed (fixed, in legal parlance) whether or not you register the work. However, you must register the work to bring an infringement suit to court. If you use your work without registering it and then find it was infringed, you would have to register the work to fight the infringement.

Similarly, a copyright notice is not required to appear with your work but is advised by many legal professionals. The reason for this is quite logical—if you do not state publicly that you own the work, an infringing user of the work can claim they were not aware of your copyright. Most commercial communications have some sort of copyright information for this reason. Copyright is usually written as the letter *c* with a circle around it. Although this designation is widely used, it is not actually an official symbol.

You must register your work to receive statutory damages. The idea of statutory damages is that if your work is duplicated without permission, it is difficult to determine in court the values of copies in terms of lost revenue. Because of this, statutory damages assign an amount per work—up to $150,000 each in some cases—instead of using a possible future sales scenario. Statutory damages have been criticized because of their frequent use by corporate copyright holders to sue for such large sums that an individual accused of infringement is usually not in a position to risk potentially losing a court battle and will settle the claim regardless of how strong the evidence may or may not be (see Figure 6–4).

The natural author of a work is granted copyright for 70 years after death. If the work was created for a company (see Work-for-Hire) or otherwise has a corporate owner, the copyright is good for 90 years from date of publication or 120 years from creation. These terms were extended by 20 years when the Copyright Term Extension Act of 1998 was passed into U.S. law. This was done in large part to protect several well-known copyrights, such as Disney's Mickey Mouse character, that would have become *public domain*—though still protected under trademark of the Walt Disney Company—without an extension in place.

## Infringement and Fair Use

Infringement is the term used when an individual or a company uses a copyrighted work without permission of the owner. Fair use is the legal term for using a copyrighted work without permission, but in a manner that is allowed because the infringement does not rise to the level of harming the original work. For example, the *New York Times Book Review* could take a passage from a copyrighted work to aid in the criticism of the work, but not reprint the book in its entirety. The excerpt would likely be judged fair use of the work, but the full reprint would be almost certainly be infringement. The courts are also free to consider other factors beyond the four tests as they see fit for an infringement case. The standards used to determine whether the situation is, in fact, infringement are the four legal tests for *fair use*.

The first fair use test is the nature of the original and infringing work. Is your artwork something that takes talent and years of work, or could it be coincidence that your work looks, sounds, or otherwise appears to be similar to the alleged infringement? Does the new work transform the original work to a new meaning or art form? A key focus of this fair use is the level of creativity. Designers can appreciate more than most, of course, that all creative work is not created equal. Art that is truly groundbreaking or takes the form of expression in a new direction is more likely to be protected than something that is only modestly different from other works of the type. When pop artist Andy Warhol painted Marilyn Monroe in bright colors, there was obviously a new creative

figure |6–4|

Black Keys Poster

Firm: Methane Studios

Designer: Robert Lee

direction on display. If you painted a modern movie star in the same manner, the level of creativity would be considerably less and therefore make infringement harder to prove.

The purpose of the infringement also matters. If you use the signature style of the *Lexus* national magazine ads in a campaign to sell BMWs, you are more than likely subject to an infringement case because your work is intended to be directly competitive to the original. If you use the same style to promote safe driving and warn against the dangers of driving under the influence, you are not as likely to be subject to an infringement case, though it still could happen. If your work is a parody, this test is usually the one that will become your defense in an infringement case. Parody is protected by law as free speech and therefore not easily ruled infringement. However, the point at which a parody is as similar to a brand as to create consumer confusion or devalue a brand name it may cross the legal line and lose this protection.

The amount of the original work used in the infringement is also considered. For example, you could not download the screenplay to *The Godfather* and use a word processor to replace the names of each character to create a new story. Although the characters' names would differ, your new work would be found to be substantially similar and infringe against the original author of the work. However, if you used one of many famous lines from the movie, *"I'm gonna make him an offer he can't refuse,"* for example, in a movie that was completely different in situations, action, characters, and style, you would be far less likely the subject to an infringement suit and it would probably be considered fair use if it made it to the courts. This test centers on what is considered the "heart" of the work—the core thing that makes the work unique and desirable. If that heart is found in one line of a 200-page book or 10 seconds of a 2-hour film, the courts could still rule the use as infringement.

The last consideration of an infringement is the effect on the market for the original work. If the infringement can be seen as lessening the demand or opportunity to earn revenue from the original work, there is a stronger legal case. This is another reason why copying digital files has become a major issue in copyright litigation. In a digital copy, the duplicate is the exact same thing as the original. It can be argued, therefore, that having millions of copies of equal quality in circulation substantially damages the value of the original file. An infringement that is not an exact duplicate, however, may not rise to this level. For example, the 1977 movie *Star Wars* is conceptually based on Akira Kurosawa's earlier film *The Hidden Fortress*. Although the general idea of a hero with two hapless sidekicks trying to rescue a princess might be in common, it would be very difficult to prove that licensing revenue of *The Hidden Fortress* was negatively affected by the release of *Star Wars*. While there may not be a strong infringement case anyway, as the films are unique in many ways, the lack of financial damage to the original would further weaken the case.

## Q&A Ask the Pros:
## Core Clients
## John Fisher, Sockeye Creative

**Q: Does every successful firm take mundane, traditional design work to pay the bills?**
A: You have got to keep in mind that to do really creative work, you have to have accounts that just pay the bills. What makes you successful though is an account that not only pays the bills but forms a good relationship. It is more about finding a company that aligns with your values. You have still got to love what you do.

# Trademarks

While copyright protects works of art, identity work is more likely to fall under the other intellectual property distinction, trademarks. The trademark must differentiate the product or service
offered from others on the market and can be used by individuals, partnerships, or corporations. A
trademark includes product names and can include other ways of communicating that help draw a
clear distinction in the consumer's mind. The Internet domain name or the company name is not,
however, automatically trademarked by its use for business purposes. If you own XYZCompany.
com, the name XYZ Company is not necessarily trademarked and could be challenged by competitors that do not own the domain but operate under the name otherwise. Similarly, your business
registration of XYZ Company does not guarantee that the domain name is available to you.

Unlike copyright, a trademark is renewable. As long as the proper paperwork is filed, the trademark is effectively valid as long as it is in use. Similar to a copyright, the trademark does not have
to be registered with the government. If the company is claiming something as a trademark but
has not registered, the ™ designation is used to denote that the mark is being used for this purpose. Once the trademark is registered, the ® symbol is used to denote *registered trademark.*

Unlike copyright, trademark is not limited to duplication or modification of the fixed work. The
standard for trademark infringement is, generally, whether the consumer could be confused by
the infringing work, and think it is the original trademark company, product, or service (see
Figure 6–5). The greater the number of customers a company might have across various demographic, social, and economic groups—the mass market global appeal of McDonalds, for example—
the more broadly this consumer confusion might apply. There may not be a McDonalds in a
20-person town in Wyoming, but you could not use a giant M on the sign for the hamburger stand
you open there because prospective consumers might pull off the interstate expecting to find the
famous chain. This does create the problem that global brands with mass market advertising such
as television must police their trademarks around the world. It might not seem reasonable to a

Consumer Whore Parody Logo ©2000 Kieron Dwyer   www.LCDcomic.com

figure |6–5|

In 2000, Starbucks sued artist Kieron Dwyer for his
parody of Starbucks well-known mermaid logo. The
judge agreed that the logo was protected as parody
but ruled that sales of t-shirts and bumper stickers
with the parody would only result from the similarity
to the original logo, and therefore was a trademark
infringement. The case is now settled and Dwyer can
no longer sell merchandise with the logo or display the
logo on his own Web site.

restaurant owner in Perth or a coffee shop in Rome that giant Ms and green circles are the exclusive property of American companies, but this coverage does increase the challenge, demand, and required skill of creating truly unique brands that can travel.

Trademarks used without registration are regional and can only be enforced if the company is conducting business in the area of the alleged infringement (see Figure 6–6). For example, a landscaping company operating in Miami under the name The Cutting Edge Lawn and Landscape would not be able to enforce their trademark in Phoenix, unless they could prove they have active customers and are conducting business there. The Internet does not automatically make the region—called a *zone*—enforceable unless the same standard is met. A seller of hats with a website called MyWesternHatStore.com could not claim the entire nation as their zone, and could only make a trademark claim against a seller at a mall outside of Chicago unless they could prove they are getting repeated interest—customer inquiries, sales, returns—from the Chicago area.

Once a trademark is registered, the entire country is the zone. The reason for this is that an unregistered trademark would be a state level case, whereas a federally registered trademark would not. The identity developed for a client must go through the formal process of a trademark search—research to determine whether the mark is unique—and then the registration process to be used without fear of infringement claims. A law office specializing in patent, copyright, and trademark generally conducts this search but much of the legwork and initial research steps can increasingly be done online.

With a registered trademark to use in business, the firm or the individual owning the mark must police infringement of the work. Although a trademark owner is not often going to dedicate an entire business to watching for infringement, it is important not to allow unauthorized use of the trademark. When an infringement is found, the trademark owner may send a *cease and desist* letter requesting the infringing use be stopped and removed from circulation. The active policing of a trademark creates a history that can be recalled in court if an infringement later causes severe damage to the mark. This is why a relatively harmless and amateur use of a world-renowned mark—the Nike swoosh, for example—will still generate interest from lawyers representing the

## TRADEMARKS

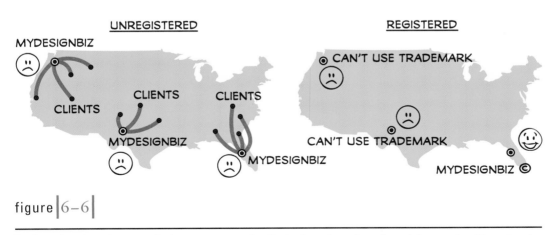

figure |6–6|

Trademark registration expands the zone, or area that the trademark can be enforced, from regional to national.

company. If Nike failed to do this policing and waited for a major firm to infringe the mark, their case would not be as strong because there would be no history of protecting their interest in—and the value of—the swoosh.

The last threat to trademark value is a problem every designer might want to face—a trademark that becomes so common and so dominant in its product category that it becomes generic. Many words used in everyday speech to mean any of a number of brands are current or former trademarks. If someone sneezes nearby, they may turn to you and ask for a Kleenex. They may or may not prefer the actual facial tissue produced by Kimberly-Clark, a major paper goods company, but the name Kleenex has become synonymous with the type of product. Another example of this phenomenon is aspirin, a German trademark until the end of World War I. At that point, the aspirin trademark, along with many assets of the old German government, were seized and resold. Today, aspirin is a term used in popular speech and means "pain relief medicine in pill form" more than any particular brand. In either case, it becomes very difficult to police infringement of a term once it is used in a broader context beyond the original owner of the trademark.

> Design firms and freelancers must be clear with clients that their identity work is not legal consulting. The client should use an attorney to handle the formal registration process. A competent attorney can advise your client on what type of intellectual property protection is most effective for the situation. For example, if your client has developed something that must remain a company secret, filing a patent—a publicly available document—would undermine their secrecy claim.
>
> As intellectual property concerns become more international in scope, there are also considerations for ensuring protection globally. Many nations have similar legal concepts in place to protect intellectual property, but their filing deadlines and requirements may be different. This is usually outside the realm of advice a design firm can give a client, so it is beneficial to establish a professional relationship with an attorney. An attorney's office may also be a good source of referrals, as many businesses speak to their attorneys about a project before they have a creative brief ready, so a reciprocal referral situation would benefit both firms.

## Patents

Most of the work produced by design firms, at least those that specialize in traditional areas of identity, print, and other business communications, is intellectual property under copyright or trademark rules. As designers with a background in graphics and branding are increasingly brought into product design and strategic work, the work may cross into the realm of invention. Work that brings something entirely new into the world is often patented, an intellectual property process that differs in some ways from the business identification of trademark or the artistic creation of copyright.

One of the more difficult areas of patents is to balance the timing of the application with the amount of information that must be disclosed. Savvy competitors will read patent applications—which are public record—as soon as they are filed, learning the inner workings of the new creation. At the same time, the filing must be done in a certain time frame or the patent could be ruled invalid. From the perspective of a design firm working on a patentable invention with a client there are legal considerations, as well. If the firm is simply executing a design—that is, the client has a complete idea and just needs it put into a 3D model or a printed format—there is no invention on the part of the design firm. In many cases though, a client may retain a design firm when the invention is in early stages or still has problems that need to be solved. At that point, the firm is acting in the role of inventor and becomes part of the patent application. If the filer of the patent, in this case the client, fails to include the firm on the application, the patent could later be invalidated. As such, it is the responsibility of the firm to make sure any invention they are participating in is properly negotiated and documented. This is not just a payment issue—though the design firm may feel justified to request some ongoing royalty from the invention—but also in the best interest of the client, as their competitors will work to find ways the patent can be circumvented.

The two major legal tests for patents are novelty and nonobviousness. Novelty, having a novel idea, simply means the invention is new and has not existed before. With over eight million inventions on file with the U.S. Patent Office, novelty may not be as simple to prove as it sounds. The next test, however, is the more difficult hurdle. The invention must be *nonobvious*. This means that if a group of people trained in the area were assembled, they would not view the invention as the next logical step in development. For example, using a manufactured panel to convert sunlight to electric power might have been in science fiction writing for years before the inventor got it to work, but a gathering of expert scientists would not have ruled that the design was simply an obvious next step in the development of electric power.

If something is too obvious, the patent office will likely rule against the filing. For example, if all the automobiles on earth were shipped with speedometers that measure miles per hour, using kilometers per hour for vehicles sold in nations that use the metric system would probably not meet the test of nonobviousness.

# CONTRACTUAL ISSUES

Intellectual property is not the only legal issue a designer should get acquainted with before working in the industry. Work agreements are legal documents as well, and contractually specify the ownership terms of the work created. Unfortunately, many designers become so interested in the project at hand that they sign one-sided contracts that are not in their best interest. Some talented designers leave the industry altogether after a few bad work arrangements sour their passion for doing the work. In this section, we discuss the most familiar pitfall—spec work—and gain an understanding of how a work-for-hire arrangement is used to transfer intellectual property rights.

## Spec Work

At some point in a designer's career, a request for services will have a different tone or wording than legitimate clients. It may the description of the newest instrument to save the world, if only the inventor could get it "down on paper" or it may be the cannot-miss brand that will rise to the Fortune 100 almost overnight if, of course, the logo was just a bit more professional. No matter how the project is described, it has a basic tenant in common—payment for design services will be paid later on the basis of some external occurrence. The client may offer to pay double your billable rate if their product succeeds, or pay just as soon as the first 100 orders arrive. Spec work may be more subtle, requiring the designer to present ideas without payment to be "considered" for an assignment. The work is thus deemed to be speculative. The practice is of doing work based on a possible future payment is known as *spec work*. Other forms of spec work include design competitions, in which only the selected design receives payment and other enticements (the promise of many referrals, for example) to create design products for commercial use without payment being made.

Spec work is frowned upon throughout the creative services industry for several reasons. The most important is that it is unethical to ask someone who has a limited number of hours to earn a living to risk that limited resource without compensation. Spec work does not allow a designer to appropriately budget time and expenses to solve a business problem, and is more of an exercise in using design software quickly than in the thinking that enables a designer to effectively communicate.

## Pro Bono versus Spec Work

Similar to other professional services, designers are often asked to do work *pro bono,* from the Latin phrase meaning "for the public good." This is not the same as spec work, but many unscrupulous businesses will use the terms interchangeably to entice a designer to work for free or less than their standard rate. Pro bono work is meant for nonprofit organizations that you feel are worthy of receiving free work to help their cause. Much like an attorney who will volunteer legal advice on occasion to people unable to afford to hire a firm, a designer might create an identity, print materials, or a website for an organization. The reason for doing this lies in the individual designer but, beyond the positive feeling of helping out, a true pro bono assignment can be valuable to build community contacts and add work to your portfolio.

It is an important distinction to understand that even though you might feel badly for the owner of a failing nightclub, a poorly financed restaurant, or a car dealer stuck with too much inventory, working for free to save them is not a pro bono assignment. If businesses such as these, or any other business owners without the resources to hire professional designers, approach you with unpaid work, it is very likely *spec work* should be avoided. As importantly, work done *pro bono* should remain a standard, contractually agreed project. Everything you would spell out in a paid design engagement, including scope, deliverables, schedule, assumptions, and use of the work should be in writing with the pro bono client. An organization requesting pro bono work that balks at signing a professional contract should be a red flag and may not be as ethical as their public image had you believe. There are many quality nonprofit organizations that could use your help, so choose carefully when working only to make a difference.

---

**Q&A Ask the Pros:**
**Creating from Life Experience**
**Sarah Hans and Partners**

*A: What advice would you give young designers?*
Q: Be interested in everything. Be a sponge. You never know what industry or what culture your next client will be from, or how some experience you had 5 years ago is going to play into helping them solve their problems today.

# Work-for-Hire

**DVD**

One of the most overlooked aspects of working for an employer is how this arrangement affects copyright. Lost in the comparison of billable rates to salary, the search for health insurance and the daunting idea of marketing yourself is the legal concept of *work-for-hire*. If a design is created in the course of employment, the copyright belongs to the company, not the individual designer, as if the company itself authored the work. A work-for-hire arrangement can also be executed between a contract designer or a design firm and the client, further reassigning the rights to the work. If the contract is intended as a work-for-hire, it must include the phrase (either as "work-for-hire" or, alternatively, "works made for hire") and must be signed before work begins on the design. This is a critical piece of the contract; as discussed in the previous section on patent filings, timing is important in intellectual property matters.

Credit given to the designer, publicly or in internal documents, does not alter a work-for-hire agreement. The author of the work remains, for most practical purposes—resale, modification, and licensing—the hiring company. As such, the contract will state if and how the designer may show the work or take credit for its creation. One example of this is software, in which work-for-hire agreements allow programmers around the world to collaborate with all intellectual property remaining with the company that employs them. Some of these software firms list these programmers much the same way a film studio credits actors, actresses, and directors at the end of a movie. Others opt to keep strict confidentiality agreements in place and do not allow the programmers to discuss any specifics of their work.

# Assignments

If a work-for-hire agreement is not in place before work starts on a project and the designer is not an employee, the intellectual property rights stay with the author of the work—the designer. This is true of a designer who is under contract to design firms, but equally the situation between design firms and their contracted clients. Without an agreement executed in advance of work with the term work-for-hire spelled out, authorship is not transferred and instead some limited use of the work is what is actually being purchased (see Figure 6–7).

If a client wants to retain all rights to the work, the closest thing to work-for-hire they can negotiate after work begins is an *assignment* of rights. By assigning authorship rights to the hiring company, the firm may act as the legal author in distributing, modifying, or generating revenue in the same way as a work-for-hire arrangement. The critical difference is in the length of the assignment. Unlike a work-for-hire, in which the authorship rights are permanently transferred, an assignment only lasts 35 years. Understandably, many designers view 35 years as the legal equivalent of "forever" in terms of ever having rights to their work again. However, if you look back at some of the major work that was done 35 years ago and consider that designers working on assignment at that time will legally own the work again, the difference between work-for-hire and assignment can be significant in terms of future revenues. As such, a designer should keep their contracts in order with other important paperwork. An assignment signed today could mean owning at least partial licensing rights to valuable work in the future. Another interesting feature of an assignment is that the rights revert to the creator of the work even if the contract expressly states otherwise. This means that a designer who signs an assignment that is not in his best interest still has an opportunity—albeit many years later—to earn additional money from the work.

figure |6–7|

Montevina

Creative Director: Kenn Fine

Art Director/Designer: Ryan McAdam

Illustrator: Nilobon Kijkrailas

Copywriter: Josh Kelly

For this irreverent wine brand, FINE created an all-handmade Web site, using analog illustrations to build a unique look and feel, and convey the personality and spirit of the winemakers.

## Nondisclosure and Noncompete Agreements

Design has increasingly become a strategic area for business and with this rise in importance comes responsibility not to disclose information about clients that could be used by competitors. Because design works across so many different areas of an organization, many designers become knowledgeable in business processes and other trade secrets that must not become public information.

To protect their interests, many clients will request designers sign a nondisclosure agreement (NDA). An NDA is a contract that simply puts in writing the information that must be kept in confidence. This may include a number of areas, from formulas to trade partners. Similarly, a design firm may require an NDA from designers so that clients can be assured that all members of the staff have agreed to keep client secrets.

A nondisclosure does not usually create a criminal offense, as piracy of intellectual property does in many jurisdictions (including U.S. federal laws). However, as a civil law area, designers who break their nondisclosure agreement may find themselves in court facing significant financial penalties.

Along with nondisclosure, a design firm or in-house creative department may try to restrict employees from working for competitors. Like an NDA, a noncompete clause is added to the employment agreement of a designer on the basis that the work will result in exposure to secrets and unique processes that should not be shared with competitors.

A noncompete clause restricts the designer from moving to a competitor of their employer. This is not a clearly enforceable area, as an employer cannot deny someone the right to earn a living. Further complicating enforcement of a noncompete agreement is the state of California. California, with its abundance of Internet, biotechnology, and other firms that rely heavily on both secrecy and skilled labor has ruled against noncompete agreements and allows them only in limited situations.

Because it could be said that all design firms are in competition with each other in some way, a noncompete suit would usually be filed only when the hiring gives one competitor a clear advantage over another. For example, if a designer with in-depth knowledge of how their employer would bid on a large prospective client, another firm could not easily hire them away to gain this knowledge and adjust their bid to win the project. An important consideration for the designer is that a noncompete is part of their employment agreement and it may be their responsibility to defend a lawsuit if they choose to change employers. As such, it is best to have the new firm review the agreement and, in some cases, even agree to pay for claims based on the noncompete clause.

---

- The creator of a new, original work is granted *copyright,* an exclusive legal right to profit from their creation.
- The four tests the courts use to determine fair use of a copyrighted work are the nature of the work, the purpose of the infringement, the amount of the original work used, and effect on the market for the original work.
- The standard for trademark infringement is generally consumer confusion between the infringing work and the original company, product, or service.
- The two major legal tests for patents are novelty—the invention is new and has not existed before—and nonobviousness—a group of people trained in the area would not view the invention as the next logical step in development.
- The practice is of doing work based on a possible future payment is known as *spec work.*
- To protect their interests, many clients will request designers sign a nondisclosure agreement, a contract that puts in writing the information that must be kept in confidence.

**THE BOTTOM LINE**

# DESIGN ASSETS

# introduction

Many designers are talented illustrators. Some learn enough photography to capture the perfect image for a project. Type design is a time-honored specialty and continues to be very important in corporate communications. As technology has revolutionized video and made the medium approachable to many more clients, designers must be able to apply it to their work. These specialties come together in a design firm, but only the largest firms would have a team that can create all of these assets at a high level. As such, there is a thriving market of images, video, type, and illustration that can be integrated into projects. In this chapter, we will look at these assets and take a closer look at the license issues in using them.

# objectives

**The products most commonly used in creative services—fonts, stock photography, and illustration.**

**Where to find quality sources of digital products and what to expect in terms of cost.**

**How digital assets are licensed and the advantages and disadvantages of each license type.**

**How many design tasks can be automated, and how this impacts your work as a designer.**

# PRODUCTS

Design, like any creative output, is generally thought of as a service business. Although frequently used as a noun, that is, "We need the creative by Thursday," what is actually being exchanged is the mental energy, manual labor, and skills of a designer to create something of value where there was only a blank sheet of paper or "Untitled-1" Photoshop file.

The creative services industry does, however, use millions of dollars of products in the course of producing the work. Images you see on websites, in magazines, or on billboards are likely to come from suppliers of photography. Typefaces of every style can be purchased for use or licensed for a single use. As digital video has supplanted older professional formats, discs of video backgrounds and common scenes can be purchased and incorporated into advertising or training materials. In each case, what was originally a service—the time and skills of a designer—is now a product. This allows designers to work more quickly, with more options, and usually with less expense than using specialists for every area of a project. In this section, we explore several common digital products in the design industry and learn how they are appropriately used.

## Photography

The right image can make all the difference in a design project. Getting that perfect shot from a contracted photographer can be very expensive and time consuming. As such, many projects will not have the budget for a professional photographer. Although the option (or temptation, depending on your point of view) is there to use a consumer-level digital camera, the more common, cost-effective, and professional approach is to buy an image from a stock photography supplier.

The variety of stock photography available to designers has exploded as digital images have replaced film. The seemingly unlimited supply means that any niche, situation, location, and type of person you may need for a project is probably available. On the downside though, this unlimited supply means sorting through plenty of images that you do not need—a time-consuming process especially when the combination of quality and price enters the equation.

On the high end of the stock market, companies like Getty Images contract some of the best photographers and photo studios in the world. Their editorial department, for example, is a resource for almost any notable event such as sports or news and can be licensed for use very quickly after it happens. The pricing of images from these firms is, understandably, on the high end of the scale as well. Although many clients can afford to absorb this cost, it may not be appropriate for all of your projects (see Figure 7–1).

figure |7–1|

A rights managed stock photograph from Getty Images.

Image Number: 200554229-002

Collection: Taxi

Credit: Adrian Myers

As you move down the cost scale, the number of stock photography options multiplies. Some stock catalogs sell images for as low as $1. There is a range of quality at lower prices, similar to bargain shopping in any other field. While you may be able to find a suitable image for many projects, top clients may not be satisfied with these photos. The other consideration in terms of price is the licensing structure. A lower-priced website might not offer the range of exclusive licenses available from more expensive providers and only sell them royalty free, meaning that your client may find their image used on the websites or marketing materials of other companies.

Stock photography suppliers use several pricing models to sell and license their catalogs. The most common variations are price per image, price per collection, and by subscription. A cost assigned to a single image is simple enough to understand, with the exception of the assignment of rights (see Licensing). A price per collection is usually sold in either downloadable or disc distribution. This type of pricing would be good if several clients needed similarly themed images, but different specific photographs. An example of a collection would be "urban fashion" or "summer holiday at the beach." The images would be thematically tied and sold less expensively than buying all the images in the collection.

Subscription services allow the designer (or design firm) the opportunity to download a set number of images per month or year at a fixed monthly or yearly cost. Some plans even are considered "all you can eat" subscriptions, meaning that your monthly fee entitles you to download all the images you desire without restriction. Although it may sound like a losing proposition for the stock supplier to allow unlimited download, the reality is that the cost per image is low enough that it is not cost-effective for most designers to spend excessive amounts of time downloading images. Subscription services also change how the cost must be passed on to clients, as the images selected from that supplier will not have a set cost. As such, the monthly fees are just a cost of doing business like the office rent or the electricity, and must be factored into the overall billable rates of the firm.

Another consideration of using a stock photography provider is research. As time consuming as finding the right image can be online, major vendors of photography often offer professional research via phone. Someone familiar with the stock libraries can help turn your description— often a condensed version of vague ideas from the client and several designers—into a smaller subset to review and try out in a layout. This is a valuable timesaver and is part of what you are paying for when you use the more professional services.

Once you have selected a few photos for your layout, a sample image called a *comp* is used in place of the full licensed version of the photograph. The comp will usually be watermarked with the logo of the stock supplier to designate the image is not yet purchased for use. These images are usually not the same quality as the final product in terms of resolution, but are good enough to communicate to the client how the finished product will appear. Once the client approves the image for commercial use, the fully licensed image is used in place of the comp.

Stock photography and the other creative products discussed in this chapter can significantly add to the cost of a project. Without careful consideration of how these images will be used and alter the budget for a job, the designer's profit can vanish. This is especially critical to freelancers, because they are typically paying for expenses out of their own hourly rates. A freelancer must keep stock resources in mind and review with the client the available budget for using these images. As your clients require exclusive or hard to find images, you may move toward licensing terms that adjust the price based on size and distribution of the creative asset. The designer must be familiar with the pricing of creative assets and make sure there are no cost surprises based on the images chosen.

Last minute changes by a client because of a misunderstanding over responsibility for stock costs can wreck a project, cause missed deadlines, and lose an opportunity for repeat business and referrals.

## Fonts

Many design students take the fonts they use for granted. Most design schools have a decent selection of typefaces installed on machines in various labs and classrooms, and it is not until later coursework that students start to push the limits of these fonts and start downloading and installing their own. Even then, many schools have policies against adding fonts to machines, so it becomes an exercise in frustration to use interesting type on their own computers or laptops and then transfer the files to the school machines. As with most lessons in a design program, the student is generally more immersed in the specific technique, look, or message of their work and the specifics of licensing are the furthest thing from consideration. After graduation, fonts can no longer be taken for granted as included with tuition and, especially for freelancers and small design shops, can be very expensive.

Type foundries sell millions of dollars of fonts each year, and for good reason—exceptional typography makes a huge difference in the quality of a design project. Seemingly every conceivable style of type is available, from replicas of engravings found on eighteenth-century pirate ships to fonts that render well on a monitor because of their pixel exact measurements. While many of these fonts are free, and freely available, there is still a thriving market for professional quality type. Free fonts, like free anything, can be very good—the work of perhaps an undiscovered type design genius—but can just as easily be low quality and poorly done. Because of this divide in quality, the compressed deadlines of professional design work, and the high cost of having a paying job print, render on screen, or animate incorrectly, quality fonts are still essential and generally considered worth the price.

Fonts are licensed for use. As a designer, it is your responsibility (along with your employer) to own the right to use the fonts as you do. Like stock photography, this can alter your budget significantly if you are accustomed to "borrowing" fonts from other designers or buying a single license of a font for a 10-person design firm. Top quality fonts can sell for more than $100 and type collections can easily cost thousands of dollars. As the font is software and its use is governed by a license agreement, there is a legal risk to using fonts without purchasing them.

Similar to hiring a professional photographer, a type designer can create a truly unique, exclusive typeface for a client. This commissioned work can be very expensive, so the more practical option is often to limit the exclusivity of a typeface in some way, such as a certain amount of time. This gives the client the exclusive they may desire—such as using a unique holiday typeface for the season—while giving the type designer or foundry the right to sell the rights the following year for additional profit on their work.

Another consideration of selecting a font, much like stock photography, is the rights to use granted with the license. Font licensing can be difficult to understand because it is usually done per *device*, not per computer. For example, if a font grants the right to use five devices and you use one Mac, one PC, a color printer, a large format plotter, and a high-speed laser printer at your design workstation the entire license would be used. In other words, by the terms of the license, the next additional printer you installed and used with the font or the next workstation you used with a copy of the font would need additional licenses.

Once the work is created, the end user license agreement for the font must allow for the distribution of the project. There are some caveats in these licenses that can cause the project to go over budget in a hurry. For example, if you distribute the project as a PDF that can be edited, the font may need to be licensed for use on each machine that will edit the document. The same project distributed with editing disabled (view and print only) may not need additional licenses. The type foundry House Industries, for example, allows two options for non-editable PDF distribution—a small fee per file that uses the font or an annual fee to license the font for this purpose. This is in addition to the standard license to use the font on the designer's workstation and printers. In most cases, embedding a font to send to a printer or service bureau does not require additional licenses.

Although the fees associated with using professional fonts will seem expensive when you first use them, remember that the type foundries must charge for the use of their products to stay in business. A good type foundry can be a key business resource for your design practice, so work with them to understand their license terms and remember the cost of the product will be, and should be, passed on to the client in some form. Whether you explicitly add a line item in your invoices or add the cost of your font collection to your base expenses, good quality type products are essential to quality work and getting the proper licenses should not be an optional cost for a professional firm.

For simplicity, we use the terms *font* and *typeface* interchangeably in this section. Technically, the typeface is the collection of letterforms and is legally protected creative work. If you draw an alphabet by hand in a manner not previously created, you created a typeface. A designer, therefore, cannot legally alter a typeface unless the foundry or type designer grants permission to do so.

A font is the computer rendering of the typeface and is generally offered, as other software, by means of an end user license agreement. Fonts are generally licensed per machine or group of machines and cannot be freely exchanged between designers without additional licenses.

# Video

Video has not traditionally been part of the creative output of a graphic design firm. Graphic firms mainly focused on print work, identity, and related branding issues. The immense expense and complexity of video work meant that only the largest marketing budgets would extend their brands in a meaningful way into moving images. With television as the primary vehicle for video, national advertising campaigns were the most likely use for video. As such, many of the smaller design firms that make up the vast majority of all professional creative work were not equipped—both in skills and hardware—to script, shoot, and edit video.

As the Internet has made video distribution accessible to everyone and desktop editing applications approach the quality offered only by the major studios in the 1990s, video is now a critical piece of the brand message. The same issues designers face with other integrated marketing, such as consistent message and positioning, must now be applied in creative ways to video. Just as many design firms now routinely oversee or actively participate in Internet site design projects, video and motion graphics expands what design firms offer and presents a new business opportunity.

Another layer of cost, legal, and licensing issues comes with the opportunity present in adding video to the creative services mix. Custom video work can be very expensive and will require a significant portion of a client's creative budget. However, many uses of video such as integration in websites do not really require custom, or even exclusive, images. Video, like still photography, can be purchased as stock footage for incorporation in a project. Many vendors are available to preview, select, and download video online for use in creative projects. Like stock photography and type, there are licenses to consider. Understanding how this footage can be used and how your use affects cost is likely worth the opportunity to add video to your services.

Video footage can be purchased as separate clips to edit together into a meaningful sequence or as fully produced commercials that only require some basic edits such as titles. In either case, the licensing for video is similar—and based on—that of photography.

Another legal issue of video work that is easy to overlook is right to use the audio tracks embedded in the piece. If a client requires sound, especially music, for any video work the track requires a separate license to be legally distributed.

Modern editing software makes it very easy to grab a track or two from your music library and add it to a video, but doing so does not allow you to distribute it. For this reason, stock music sources are widely available with music, sound effects, and voiceovers with the rights cleared and ready to use in your video project. Some video distribution websites, such as YouTube, also make music tracks available to insert in a video, but the selection is much more limited than doing your own research.

# Illustration

Illustration and line art can also be licensed from stock resources. The license types are the same as photography with rights managed and royalty free being the two most common. A firm will often license illustrations created by their designers in the same way rather than sell all rights. The illustration comps, or versions that were not approved by the client, also revert to the designer or the firm. This is important in designing identity materials, as these are usually line art, rather than photography, based. An identity package would be sold to the client for their unrestrained use, but comps that lead up to the final logo may serve as a basis for future work in other industries.

In designing identity materials, it is important to consider that the illustration and typeface may require different licenses. If the lettering on a project is done by hand (or otherwise manually, as with illustration software) in a unique typeface, the text becomes part of the illustration and would usually be licensed as such. If the client requested the text be developed further into an entire typeface and have a font created for use in other projects, this work would be billed separately.

Design software now allows the creation of line art from photographs. This use of digital "tracing" is generally not an allowed use of commercial photography, and the change in format would invalidate the license of the original photograph. At that point, it may be more of an ethical dilemma than legal issue, as today's tools allow designers to modify and mix photographs and illustrations beyond recognition. As assets are selected for a project, a principal or the legal counsel of the design firm should review the intended use. License infringement could cause the firm, or the client, expensive legal processes to dispute the use of the work. Although the organization Creative Commons does encourage the licensing of work for remixing, mash-ups, and other blending of artwork, major distributors of commercial grade design assets have yet to create licenses for this purpose.

## LogoWorks

Orange Frog Productions is a company that does lighting and production design for theater. They also do some architectural lighting projects as well as video production. The original logo was taken from an old postcard (a frog in a top hat, overcoat, carrying an umbrella), so the client wanted to freshen it up a bit. Three designers were assigned and the concepts shown here, and final selected logo, were the result (see Figures 7–2 to 7–3f).

figure |7–2|

Final logo.

Client: Orange Frog Design.

Credit: LogoWorks

(a)

(b)

(c)

(d)

(e)

(f)

figure | 7–3a to 7–3f |

Comps created during the redesign of Orange Frog Productions logo.

Client: Orange Frog Productions.

Credit: LogoWorks

# LICENSING

As we have seen in the previous sections, one of the main concerns of using creative assets—stock photography, font libraries, video footage, illustrations—is the legal right to use the product for its intended purpose. Licensing creative assets affects the cost of the product, sometimes substantially. If done improperly, licensing issues can cause additional expense, embarrassment, and time-consuming corrections before the project. In this section, we look at the most common types of licenses and understand when each is appropriate for a project.

## Royalty Free

The simplest license to understand and one of the most widely used for creative assets is *royalty free*. A royalty is money paid to the creator of a work for its continued use in a commercial pursuit. If you take a photograph and require that a company pay you a small fee each year to continue using the photo in their advertising, they are paying you a *royalty*. Thus, royalty free means the creative asset can be used for continued commercial use without additional payment, or free of ongoing royalties.

Royalty free images are not, however, free for commercial use. Digital images are generally priced based on the size of the image in pixels. The larger the image, the more pixel data it contains, the better it will look when printed and the more image information available for editing. It stands to reason, therefore, that a high resolution royalty free image is more expensive than low resolution—often listed on websites as "web resolution" to indicate 72 dpi, the resolution of a standard monitor. From a leading stock photography provider, this could be a difference of several hundred dollars for a single image.

In recent years, royalty free images have become a rapidly expanding market and prices have fallen considerably. Now, only the best providers with extensive networks of professional photographers—Veer, Getty, Corbis, and Jupiter, for example—can command a premium for their royalty free images. Others have filled their catalogs with work from amateur and less accomplished professional photographers and offer these images for as low as $1.

Royalty free images can be used many times after purchase and for many projects. This is an especially flexible option for backgrounds and more generic imagery that may be used in different industries. For example, a photo of a couple walking on the beach could be used by a firm in a brochure for a boutique hotel and on a website for an insurance company. Although the uses are unrelated, the designer is licensed to use the image in this manner.

However, many royalty free images do restrict the number of designers per license using the image. For example, an image from Getty Image that is licensed as royalty free can have a maximum of ten users. For most smaller design shops, this limit is inconsequential. A larger firm that is compiling a catalog of images for use across multiple offices would need to contact Getty or their royalty free image provider of choice and discuss license options for such a large group of users.

Royalty free design assets are relatively inexpensive and easily accessible. They provide a lot of flexibility and the ability to spread the cost of the image across multiple clients. These advantages are significant, but there is a downside. Royalty free images are nonexclusive, and there is a chance that your client may find their image used by another firm—even direct competitors.

This is not a minor issue, as the elements of the marketing campaigns of any industry leader or respected brand are subject to imitators. The use of royalty free images or illustration could add to this problem, as unscrupulous competition could acquire the same elements to draw unsuspecting customers.

Finally, the designer's license to use the royalty free image is usually not transferable, so there is no way to give away or sell the image to another designer once the project is over. This effectively means that a royalty free collection of images may be useful to have on hand but not tangibly add value to the firm. The valuation and sale of a design firm is outside the scope of this text, however, because of the complex accounting and legal issues involved.

## Rights Managed

The term *rights managed* is used throughout the industry to mean the artist, photographer, or an organization contracted by the creator of the work will monitor the use of the work. In contrast to royalty free, rights managed assets may require ongoing payments and are priced based on several factors instead of using size in pixels as the primary factor.

Rights managed assets are licensed *per use* and do not grant broad permission to use the image, illustration, or video for multiple projects or clients. Using a formula, the grantor of the license takes into consideration how the asset will be used, how long the asset will be used, and what the distribution of the project will be. The core idea behind rights managed images is that the larger the image, the longer it is used, and the larger the circulation of the work featuring the image, the more the photographer or artist should earn.

For this section, we will use the price calculator available from Getty Images to compare the cost of a rights managed image of a skier in Switzerland (Image 200554229-002 from Taxi) based on how the image will be used. Costs are accurate as of August 2007, but can vary widely among images from Getty. This example is for illustrative purposes only, and the image was chosen at random by the author. The terms that affect the price of the license are shown in bold.

**Example 1:**

The image of the skier used for a **tourism** billboard campaign of **up to 5 billboards** in the **United States** with the image occupying **up to one half the area** of the advertisement would, for a **six-month** license, cost $2,110. Adding several nations in Europe to the licensed territory added approximately $600.

**Example 2:**

The image of the skier used for an **internal presentation** within a company in the **tourism** industry in the **United States** would cost $265 for a **one-month** in circulation license.

**Example 3:**

The image of the skier used as a **full-page** advertisement in a **print magazine** with a circulation of **up to 2 million** (*BusinessWeek, Forbes,* or Fortune, for example) in the **United States** for a company in the **tourism** industry, would cost $3,945 for a **one-month** license.

**Example 4:**

The image of the skier licensed with a Web Flexible License Pack would cost $4,795. This license pack covers unlimited web use within the United States, in the tourism industry for one year, including promotional email, advertisements, corporate or promotional site, and mobile device. Adding several nations in Europe did not change the license price in this example.

Rights managed does not guarantee the image or asset will be exclusive. In fact, the vendors of these images sell exclusive rights to an image separately. Exclusivity may be granted in several forms. Each pricing variable in a rights managed image roughly translates to an attribute that can be made exclusive. For example, the vendor may sell the exclusive right to use the image in a given territory (the United States, Bermuda, etc.) or in a given industry (tourism, banking, computer hardware) or specific media (television, print, etc.). The duration of the exclusive is generally set for the same amount of time as the purchased license—a one-month license with a one-month exclusive, for example.

If all of these factors matter to the client, they can purchase total exclusivity for a given amount of time or negotiate to purchase the image outright if the vendor will sell. A multinational company that wants to use an image without risk of competitors using the same image across multiple forms of media, in many territories might purchase total exclusive rights. It will cost a significant amount of money, but if the image is set in Antarctica or features several models in a recognizable location, the cost may still end up lower than hiring a photographer, paying for a custom photo shoot, the requisite travel and the model releases required.

# Rights Ready

Getty Images is one of the leading vendors of photography, illustration, and video footage and includes large catalogs of archived works and editorial teams to provide images from news and current events. In the fall of 2006, Getty introduced a new license type, called *rights ready,* in an attempt to make rights managed assets easy to manage. Because this form is being closely watched by other vendors and may become a third standard (along with royalty free and rights managed), we will briefly introduce it here.

Rights ready images are licensed for a certain type of use, but not as specifically as most rights managed assets. For example, a rights ready category is **Print Ad or Display Use**. This license covers many forms of print advertising, including billboards, tradeshow displays, or store decoration. This is broader than a rights managed image, for which each of these uses would be licensed independently of each other or have to be grouped into a "license pack" to combine the licenses into a single, easily purchased item.

The rights ready license is assigned to one client and is not to be reused across multiple clients in the manner allowed by a royalty free license. However, additional use of the image in the same medium for the same client does not require an additional license. The license extends 10 years from purchase. This would allow a client to use the image for this long in the same medium without additional license fees. A rights managed image of this duration would likely be considerably more expensive. However, a rights managed image does have the option for purchasing exclusivity. Exclusive use is not currently part of the rights ready license model.

## Creative Commons

The commercial creative asset providers operate by retaining the rights to a work—photography, illustration, etc.—and then licensing it for commercial use. On the other end of the spectrum are thousands of artists in many fields who do not license their work by any of the methods we discussed and are not represented by an agency. For reasons ranging from the greater good of the planet to hobbyists that do not want to make a career of their passion, these artists own the copyright to their work but do not wish to sell or license it.

This polarity between established professionals who can command thousands for a single image to amateurs who only use their work for their own enjoyment leaves a void in how artwork can be distributed, combined, and reused. This is the basis for Creative Commons, an organization that licenses works of many types—from music to poems to photos—in ways that are not well served by the established agencies but more formal than simply keeping the art to yourself. Creative Commons seeks to allow content creators to retain the rights they want while publicly stating how their work can be used. This is done via the Internet and through *metadata*, information embedded in documents, and photographs that contain authorship information. This allows artwork to flow from user to user and gain a wide audience, but not leave the control of the artist altogether. A photographer building their reputation might not be able to gain representation through a leading stock house, but could attach a Creative Commons license to each photo to spread their work without consenting to commercial use.

The Attribution license lets anyone interested use your work, or even base new work off of yours, but stipulates that proper credit must be given. There is no exchange of money in this situation, but the designer can use the photo or illustration if credit is given to the creator. An artist who does not want his work used for commercial purchases can choose that option for their license. A designer could conceivably use an image marked attribution noncommercial for a project, but only for pro bono work for a nonprofit company.

- As you narrow your choices between several images, a comp—or watermarked low-resolution version of the photograph—can be used in a layout until the client approves the final piece and the rights to the image are purchased.
- Providers of digital assets offer different license types of varying expense and application, including royalty free, rights managed, and rights ready.
- A font is a software and its use is governed by a license agreement. There is a legal risk to using fonts without purchasing the rights to do so.
- A design firm will often license illustrations to clients rather than sell all rights, allowing them to reuse the illustration on future client work.

**THE BOTTOM LINE**

# 8

## YOUR OWN FIRM

# introduction

The ultimate career goal of many designers is to start their own professional practice. Although this could take the form of working alone or becoming a partner in an international firm, the more likely scenario is a small business commonly referred to as a design firm. Though the business may never grow larger than eight or ten people, the work produced can be high profile and well regarded. The work is not the only consideration, however, as a firm is a small business and must deal with myriad tax, legal, and employment issues like any other. In this section, we look at the most common legal structures of a design firm, and learn how specialists in key business areas can help a designer start and grow their practice.

# objectives

**The major legal structures available for starting your own business.**

**Advantages and disadvantages of business partnerships and incorporating.**

**When you need an accountant, what they will be able to do, and how they will help your business as it grows.**

**The role of an attorney and the importance of proper legal protections to a design business.**

**About the insurance policies commonly carried by a design or creative services firm.**

**Commonly used business models for creative firms.**

**The challenges and opportunities in new business models such as virtual firms and cooperatives.**

# STRUCTURE

For a designer who gets up the nerve to venture down the long road of building a business, the structure of the firm might be the last thing on the priority list. There are clients to find, please, and keep. There are new bills to pay that may never have occurred to someone who has not owned a business—yes, the liquid soap in the restroom is *your* expense now. The computers in the office that may have been coveted for iconic industrial design now seem unreasonably expensive and require the new entrepreneur to keep them running years after the coolness has worn off. The lights have to stay on. Employees, even if you have only yourself and your business partners, need somewhere to park when they arrive to work. And of course, they need an office at which to arrive.

Around item one hundred on the to-do list might be the idea of incorporating. The business selected a name—that probably was the fun part—and registered it so you can cash the checks that you plan to receive. To many small business owners starting out, that filing—usually a state *fictitious name filing* or *d/b/a* (doing business as) to allow you to use your business name—is all the paperwork needed to get rolling (see Figure 8–1).

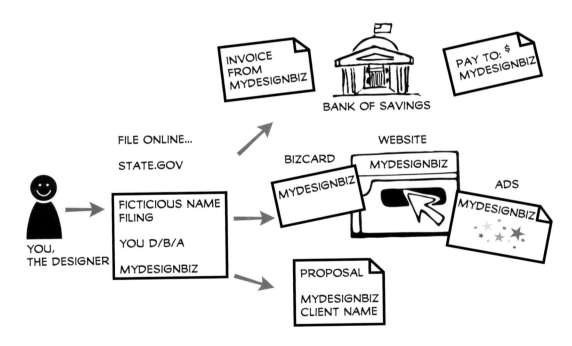

A FICTICIOUS NAME FILING ALLOWS YOU TO USE THE
NEW BUSINESS NAME ON PROPOSALS, INVOICES,
MARKETING MATERIALS, AND CASH CHECKS MADE

figure 8–1

A fictitious name filing allows you to use your new business name on proposals, invoices, marketing materials, and even bank accounts to cash checks made out to the business.

Lawyers, accountants, and anyone else who has ever run a business will advise you—and I strongly recommend you seek professional advice on all the topics in this section—that you need to think about legally structuring your firm first, before the clients and paychecks and awards and headaches of owning your own firm consume your days. Naming yourself "My Creative Firm" might allow you to cash a check made out to that name, but it will not help you with two areas that have enormous long-term consequences on both you, as an owner of the business, and your firm. Those two areas are taxes and legal protection.

There are a number of structures you can choose, each with its own advantages and disadvantages. Your first corporate filing will likely not be your last, and you may find your original business plan and the structure created for it was completely off base from the reality of how your firm looks a year later. With that said, the more you understand your options before you go into the business, the less likely you will have to make time consuming and costly changes as the firm matures. Looking even further ahead, your structure may be suitable for taking on additional partners or even selling your firm. Long-term goals for creative services firms run the gamut from simple income replacement for an artist fed up with a 9-to-5 routine to talented self-promoters intent on building a multiple practice area firm with offices in ten major design centers. Whatever your personal goals in starting your firm, choosing the correct structure will help you reach them.

Artists often shy away from areas of law, accounting, and other major structures of business and can be cynical that the system will work for them. In the years following numerous widely publicized corporate scandals—Enron, MCI, Arthur Andersen—filing for incorporation can make someone new to owning a business feel they are becoming part of the problem. Although certainly understandable to be concerned about abuses of the system, keep in mind that structures such as corporations are in place to protect you as a business owner. Without corporations, you would have to risk your personal assets and in some cases even your future earnings to go into business for yourself. Take full advantage of this protection. When viewed as an opportunity to shield your personal assets, you may find yourself less averse to learning more about "the system" and may have more confidence to pursue clients and do your creative work.

# Sole Proprietor

The simplest form of business formation is a sole proprietorship. This means the business is registered with the applicable state offices as having a single owner. Sole proprietorships afford the least amount of legal protection of the business structures we discuss in this chapter. The owner of the business is personally liable for debts, and if the business is sued, the owner's assets may be at stake.

# BUSINESS STRUCTURE: SOLE PROPRIETORSHIP

EASY SETUP                                    NO LEGAL PROTECTION

NO PARTNERS                                   CANNOT ISSUE STOCK

NO REQUIRED SHAREHOLDER                       LIMITED TAX LOOPHOLES
MEETING

NO DOUBLE TAXATION

figure |8–2|

A sole proprietorship is the most simple business structure, but does not protect owners in the same way as more involved forms, such as corporations.

The advantage of a sole proprietorship is simplicity (see Figure 8–2). The profit of the business becomes part (or all, if this is the only income source) of the owner's personal income. There are no complicated forms to fill out, no quarterly filings, and in most cases the business owner can keep track of income and expenses with simple home accounting software. With no stockholders, partners, or other owners, the sole proprietor is free to manage the business as they wish; the responsibility for success or failure of the business is owner's alone.

The sole owner may miss some tax tricks corporations can use to keep money from immediately being taxed as profits—such as retained earnings, as we will discuss later in this chapter—but do avoid the so-called *double taxation* that owners of corporations must pay. Double taxation means that an owner of a corporation is, as the name implies, taxed twice on their earnings. First, the corporation must pay taxes. The remaining profit, to the extent that it is passed on to the owner as income, is taxed again under the same personal tax formulas you are familiar with from having a regular job. Because a sole proprietorship is not a corporation, the income is only taxed once at a rate based on the owner's earnings. If the business is full time and does not earn a tremendous profit, this can mean quick work of taxes and a relatively low tax rate. The advantage of having business income taxed directly as personal income disappears, however, when someone with a good salary starts to earn additional money freelancing. At that point the business income may push them into a high tax rate and end up costing them more than they anticipated.

As a designer, the sole proprietorship may be appealing, because it is the simplest and least paperwork intensive way to be in business. You essentially declare yourself a business, file with the state, and start adding your profits to your own bottom line. This structure is limited, however, by the inability to protect you from legal entanglements and gives you limited options for reducing your tax bill. As a starting point for the business, a sole proprietorship may be adequate, but if you plan to actually build a business—adding clients, employees, equipment, and partners—you will outgrow the advantages of simplicity quickly and need to look into one of the corporate structures.

## Partnerships

Starting your own design business is no easy task, and you may wish to spread the financial risk and time commitment among several people with complimentary skills. Taking on partners is a logical choice of business structure in this situation. But while the term "partner" is used fairly often, a legal partnership is not to be taken lightly and is not always the right structure to ensure that the firm is successful. The specifics of each type of partnership can vary by state and country, so do your homework before you turn a group of people who want to start a business into an actual partnership. Let us look at some of the common forms and their strengths and weaknesses (see Figure 8–3).

### TYPES OF PARTNERSHIPS

GENERAL PARTNERSHIP, GP

LIMITED PARTNERSHIP, LP

LIMITED LIABILITY PARTNERSHIP, LLP

KEY:

 PARTNER WITH ACTIVE MANAGEMENT ROLE

PARTNER WITH ONLY FINANCIAL STAKE

PERSONAL ASSETS SHIELDED FROM LIABILITY

figure |8–3|

Different partnership types, such as General Partnership, Limited Partnership, and Limited Liability Partnership, differ in how much they expose the partners to legal risks and allow for direct management by the partners.

When you hear the term "partnership" in the context of a business structure, the form that springs to mind, in which each owner shares profits, losses, and responsibilities, is actually called a *general partnership* (GP). If several friends decide to start a design business together without consulting an attorney or accountant about structuring the partnership, the shared entity would in all likelihood be a general partnership. Each new owner would be able to directly manage the business, but is also personally responsible—like a sole proprietor to a large extent—for debts or legal obligations. This can be a serious consideration, especially if you already have assets before starting your venture and do not want to lose them if one of your partners gets your firm sued. A partnership spreads the risk and reward across multiple owners, but does not—in most states—protect the owners from being held liable for the company's actions.

Another form of partnership, the *limited partnership* (or LP, as it is often designated) allows the business to have additional owners aside from the general partners. The limited partners are only liable to the extent of their investment in the firm. For example, a limited partner invests $10,000 into the business and the firm is subsequently sued in a trademark infringement. The limited partners stand to lose their $10,000 but not their personal assets. The general partners, however, could lose considerably more than their investment, including personal assets. A limited partner may be protected, but they cannot actively manage the business. This is left to the general partners.

It stands to reason that most partners in a business, design related or not, want some protection to guard their personal belongings—such as their home, cars, or bank accounts—from the seemingly unending liability that business can create. But unlike a limited partner, they also need to run the day-to-day operations of the firm to ensure its success. These requirements lead us to the next form of partnership, the LLP, or *limited liability partnership*. In an LLP, all partners can manage the business but retain some of their protection from legal liability. However, limits on the liability of the partners vary from state to state, so even an LLP can leave the partners open to certain legal actions as a result of business activities.

During the formation of the partnership, regardless of what type (GP, LP, or LLP), partners must designate how much of the business belongs to each person. This percentage will relate to profits and losses, as well as the amount of liability each partner might incur from the business. Taxes on a partnership are done much like a group of sole proprietors. Each partner receives their share of the income of the business and is subsequently taxed on that amount as personal income.

There is another form of partnership, created more recently in some states, called an LLLP, or limited liability limited partnership. This structure is intended to protect the partners of a business more fully than the LLP, but is not currently recognized by all states and is therefore more appropriate for operations within the state in which the business was formed. For example, a Florida real estate firm may choose the LLLP structure because all legal actions related to their business would take place in Florida, a state that recognizes this business structure. If your design firm plans to have out-of-state clients, consult your attorney on how well you are protected based on your partnership arrangement.

# MISSION OF BURMA

SOME SOVIET STATION - REUNION SHOW! JAN. 13, 2007  THE EARL
PRESENTED BY OK PRODUCTIONS

Mission of Burma Grenade

Firm: Methane Studios

# Inc.

The most familiar entity in business today is the corporation. Because it is so known—and the structure of many of the world's largest and most admired firms—many entrepreneurs have in mind "My Company, Inc." or "My Corporation" as they dream up a new business. The "Inc." structure, however, is just another legal form and must be considered on its advantages and disadvantages to your creative services business.

A corporation differs from a partnership in several ways, but the most important to the prospective firm owner is that your new "Inc." is a separate legal entity from you. This does not mean your

Client: Burnet, Duckworth & Palmer LLP (or BD&P), a Calgary-based law firm

Design by Sasges Inc.

Inc. gets its own driver's license, but it does mean that lawsuits—both for and against you—are the responsibility of the corporation, not you personally. The assets of owners, as shareholders of the company, are protected against debtors. This shield is important in business, as deputes with clients, suppliers, or employees can cost the company significantly.

The corporation is a complicated entity to run, but that complexity gives the owners the most flexibility as the firm gets larger. Corporations can raise money by selling stock and even form, buy, and sell other corporations. The corporate form is the most attractive if you plan to use outside investors—shareholders that will not actively take part in the business—but for most creative firms this will not be needed.

If you own a corporation, you may be subject to double taxation (see Figure 8–4). This means that the corporate profits are taxed, and then you will be personally taxed when you receive dividends

## DOUBLE TAXATION

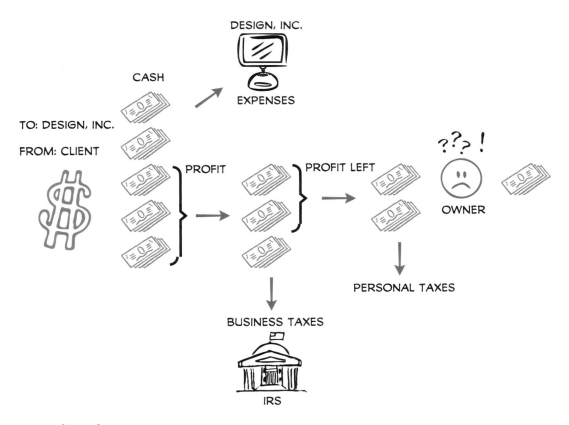

figure |8–4|

The owners of a corporation are subject to so-called double taxation, paying taxes once on the profit of the business and again when the profit is distributed to personal income.

from your company. Because of this, along with other taxes such as payroll and employment taxes you will need to be careful to use every advantage you can find to keep your tax bills from eating your profits. It may go against all business logic to reduce your profits, but that is exactly what shrewd business owners often do to avoid huge tax bills. Some of these methods are easy to understand—make sure you keep track of your business expenses, for example—and others are very complex such as depreciating assets across multiple years.

A corporation can retain earnings, or leave the profits in the business itself without distributing the money to the owners (see Figure 8–5). This allows business owners to keep money in the corporation, increasing its value and avoiding personal taxes on the entire amount the business earns each year. This sort of complicated bookkeeping can give the corporation tax advantages over partnerships, in which earnings cannot be retained. In addition, corporations in some states can elect to pass earnings directly to shareholders, avoiding the double taxation problem of this structure.

## RETAINED EARNINGS

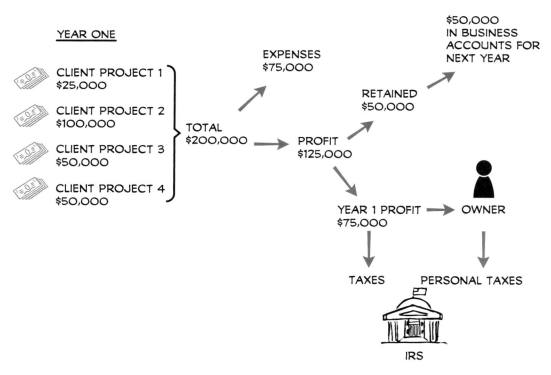

figure | 8–5 |

A corporation is not required to distribute all profits directly to owners and shareholders, but instead can retain earnings from year to year, reducing the taxes paid and increasing the value of the company.

Client: Burnet, Duckworth & Palmer LLP (or BD&P), a Calgary-based law firm

Design by Sasges Inc.

The last major advantage of corporations is that the entity can live on beyond your personal involvement in the business. The two usual ways this applies to firms such as creative businesses is the sale of the firm—and yes, creative firms are bought and sold like any other business—or the death of the owner. If you want your business to survive beyond you—Sam Walton of Wal-Mart or Henry Ford of Ford Motor Company, for example—or be sold to a large entity, the corporation is the most suitable form. For most new creative businesses, the idea of selling is not in the initial plan, but the industry has seen years in which large firms will buy up smaller, niche firms to increase their overall skills and portfolio. In some cases, large clients will buy their creative services business partner to form an in-house design group that is already very familiar with the challenges of their brand. This is not to say that a partnership or sole proprietorship could not be offered this type of opportunity, and many are, but law and accounting practices of mergers make corporations the best form for this process.

Although the corporation generally pays corporate taxes on profits, smaller and less complex companies can elect to file with the IRS (Internal Revenue Service) as an *S Corp* instead of the standard *C Corp*. The difference is that an S corporation does not pay corporate taxes and all profits are passed on to shareholders and are taxed as personal income, much like a partnership. The S form can be good option for smaller corporations such as creative firms, so ask your accountant to review this with you when you create your firm.

# Limited Liability Company (LLC)

Running the business as a corporation can be complex and time consuming, with many book-keeping and tax requirements. The main advantage for many small businesses of being a corporation is the legal protection of their assets. As such, a simplified form of corporation would be the most suitable to many small businesses, such as creative services firms. The LLC, or Limited Liability Company, is a legal structure that combines many of the most desirable aspects of corporations and partnerships.

The requirements of an LLC are considerably easier than an Inc. Because the LLC is intended for a limited number of owners, annual shareholder meetings are not required. The owners of an LLC are called "members" instead of shareholders, because an LLC cannot issue and sell stock. The personal assets of members are shielded from liability, much like the incorporated form.

Without additional filing with the IRS, an LLC is taxed as a partnership, meaning that profits are passed on to members and are taxed as personal income. This avoids the double taxation problem of a corporation. For example, if a creative firm with two equal owners (technically called *managing members* if they have an active role in the company) made a $200,00 profit, each owner would report $100,000 in personal income. However, an LLC is a very flexible form and can elect to be taxed as a corporation (or as a sole proprietorship if there is only one member).

The LLC form has become common, but is still much more recent than the standard corporation. As such, some states have slightly different treatment of LLC businesses in terms of liability protections or state taxes. Like any business structure (see Figure 8–6), your attorney and accountant should be able to advise you about the specifics of LLC filing for your state.

## A COMPARISON OF BUSINESS STRUCTURES

| | SOLO PROP. | GP | LP | LLP | LLC | INC. |
|---|---|---|---|---|---|---|
| SIMPLICITY | +++++ | +++ | | | ++ | |
| LIABILITY PROTECTION | | | ++ | +++ | +++ | +++++ |
| TAX ADVANTAGES | | | | | +++ | ++++ |
| TRANSFER OR SELL | | | | | ++ | +++++ |

figure |8–6|

Each of the business structures has advantages and disadvantages, so choose carefully with your attorney and accountant before filing the paperwork and launching your firm.

# PROFESSIONAL ADVICE

To start your own creative firm, you will need a variety of skills outside of design. Some of these will be learned as your career progresses, such as sales techniques, managing projects, and working with difficult clients. Other areas, such as accounting and taxes, are best left to experts in their respective fields. One of the more disappointing aspects of starting a design shop to many artists is that, despite the creative output or celebrity reputation that comes from award-winning work, the firm is still a business—a business that must be legally protected and go through all the routine, left-brained procedures other industries must endure. Many designers who go on their own, or with partners, learn quickly that they must get up to speed not only on accounting and

Francis Ford Coppola's La Lancha Resort

Kenn Fine, Creative Director

Nilobon Kijkrailas, Lead designer

Kirk Roberts, Flash developer

Coppola Art Department:

Gundolf Pfotenhauer, Art Director

Courtesy of Fine Design Group

bookkeeping, but also on other areas such as employment law and how to budget for office space. There are a number of professionals who can help you build your business along the way. In this section, we will look at the role of three of the more important specialists a business owner will work with when starting and growing a design firm.

# Accounting

Getting your taxes done professionally with a normal job is not a very complicated or expensive process. As an employee, you are only responsible for your own income and your employer has already paid many taxes on your behalf. Your income and deductions are all based on your individual (or perhaps combined, if you are married) situation. This type of accounting, the role that most people first utilize an accountant, is generally reactive. Your accountant reviews the year as it has already passed and makes sure you deduct all the money from your income allowed by the law. At the end of your appointment, your taxes are filed and you pay for services. In most cases, that is the extent of your interaction with your accountant for the year, and you may never hire the same person again. If your needs are not complex and you kept good records, you may forego the accountant altogether and handle everything with online services or simple tax software.

Your use of professional accounting may change considerably in your new role as a business owner. While your accountant or accounting firm may still provide end-of-the-year filing services, as your firm increases revenues you may have more filings throughout the year. Quarterly filing, or sending in estimated taxes four times a year, may be required. Your accountant therefore becomes more important in your planning. Knowing the tax laws, in some cases before they even go into effect, helps your accountant proactively recommend how to handle various financial situations that arise as your firm grows. This can become especially useful when you start hiring employees, since the costs associated with additional staff are a major expense for any creative services firm.

As logical and boring as accounting can seem to artists, you should be able to relate to this sort of strategic partnership—it is the same situation you have with your clients. Just as you can effectively manage the brands of your long-term clients more effectively because you have a deeper understanding of their business challenges, your accounting firm can help your business grow by more efficiently spending money and saving on unneeded expenses.

Questions Your Accountant Can Help You Answer:

- Is our firm making a profit?
- What is our most profitable and least profitable client?
- How many additional projects do we need before adding staff?
- If we maintain our core clients, what will the business be worth in 5 years?
- What type of project is the most profitable for our firm?
- When should we add equipment or buy office space for maximum tax advantage?
- Are our billable rates set correctly based on our expenses?

Accounting is not just bookkeeping, and modern accounting firms can often consult you on a number of different areas of business. This includes your initial business formation, because the tax implications of your business structure should be a primary concern for you and your partners. Some firms have branched into management consulting, and it is always good to have a highly trained set of eyes looking at the financial implications of your decision making. Your favorite client may not be profitable, or the type of work you do the least might actually bring you more profit than other services you continuously market. This sort of insight is something your accountant can provide over time as you build a professional relationship. At some point, your firm may decide to hire an accountant on staff, or entire department of financial people, but to start your business your best option is to find a firm that can service your new business and help you get to that point.

> Professional services like accountants can be expensive to a new firm, so do not forget to look for opportunities to trade services. Because many accounting and law firms are structurally similar to your creative business—they will probably bill you hourly or for a specific group of tasks—it is not unreasonable to trade hours with a firm that needs design, advertising, or branding help. Unless you are starting your firm with a good client base, you may not have a full slate of billable hours lined up. Trading some of those hours with other professionals keeps your expenses down and is likely to generate referral work that can help build your firm.

# Legal

Law can be the most daunting area to grasp as a new business owner. Laws govern every area of business, and many of them are not widely known. Mistakes in any area of business can create legal exposure, and the thought of being sued is enough to make many artists continue to freelance or even avoid the creative business instead of building their own firms. Lawsuits dominate business headlines, but that does not mean you need to be a lawyer to run a design firm. Like a good accountant, an attorney familiar with issues faced by creative professionals can be an important ally.

There are several areas of law that will concern you as the owner of a design firm, but all are manageable risks and do not affect the vast majority of designers. The most prominent, in large part due to online file trading and the thousands of dubious lawsuits that have resulted, is intellectual property. Although you may never become embroiled in a copyright dispute or patent infringement case, you should at least have a basic understanding of the laws in these areas and make sure your work contracts fully address these issues.

The focus of your efforts, as a business owner, to work with an attorney is to understand the applicable laws and minimize exposure to lawsuits during the course of doing your creative work. Being proactive in understanding what can and cannot be done legally will give you and your designers more confidence in working with trademarks, licensed creative assets, and other copyrighted material. For example, a client campaign might require you to use parody or perhaps

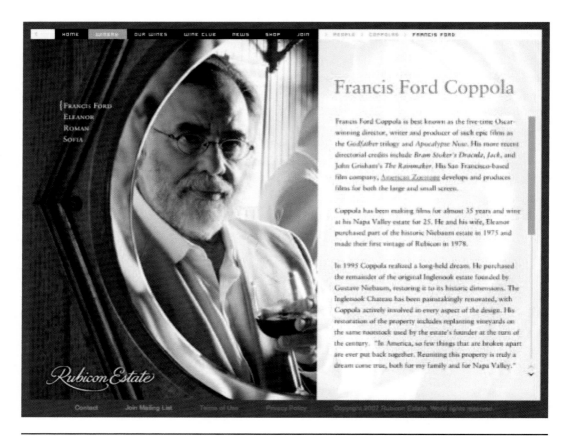

Francis Ford Coppola's Rubicon Estate

Kenn Fine, Creative Director

Tsilli Pines, Design Lead

FINE Production Team

Coppola Art Department:

Gundolf Pfotenhauer, Art Director

images from another era. In either case, there is an extensive body of case law that will direct your work and keep your firm from future legal issues. Reviewing the project with your attorney should give you more, not less, creative freedom because the nagging fear that your work is over some legal line is removed from the process.

At a minimum, your attorney should review contracts, proposals, and any binding documents signed with clients, suppliers, employees, or partner firms.

# Insurance

Even though the lawyers can protect you from some negative consequences of business, there are numerous areas that still require an extra level of certainty. Business insurance allows you to keep the firm running even when unforeseen circumstances occur. While there is no single policy that frees your mind of everything that can go wrong with your new firm, having proper insurance can save the firm from closing its doors in some situations that, despite your advance planning, throw the balance sheet off or the business plan out the window.

The most surprising thing about business insurance to new business owners is the number of areas that can, or should, be covered (see Figure 8–7). In this section, we will explore just a few common policies, but like a good attorney or accountant, you would be well served to find an insurance agent to work with as you plan, start, and continue to grow your firm.

## INSURING A DESIGN FIRM

FIRE

FLOOD

THEFT

HEALTH

INJURY/WORKERS COMP.

ERRORS AND OMMISSIONS
(E&O)

EQUIPMENT

COMPANY VEHICLES

figure |8–7|

There are many different areas of business that insurance can protect.

Health insurance is very important to many employees. In some respects, health insurance has come to be synonymous with job benefits—though benefits generally include things like a retirement saving plan—and the dividing line between contract labor and full-time employment. As a business owner, you will have a number of options in terms of the depth of coverage you wish to provide employees and how much of it you want to cover as part of the cost of doing business. It is no secret that insurance such as this is expensive, and it can be a difficult decision as your firm grows to start adding benefits. The better package you offer, the better employees you may attract and the better, faster, or more efficient your firm should be. The flip side is, of course, that benefits reduce profits and you must generate a consistent profit to keep your doors open. Some creative firms, especially those with mostly young staff, opt not to carry group health benefits until the firm is established and can afford it. Others understand that talented designers get sick too, as do their spouses and children, and making an art director pay their own medical bills entirely is not reasonable or a good way to retain quality staff.

A design firm may be full of equipment with great industrial design, but they are not generally full of heavy industrial machinery that would cause you suspect your firm is a dangerous place to work. Regardless, if you have employees, you have the potential for injury. Workers Compensation insurance covers the wages of your employee when out of work because of injury on the job. Although you probably took "Worker's Comp" for granted at your previous employer, as a business owner you will have to carry this coverage. Injuries happen in the workplace with surprising frequency, and even if your employee only misses one afternoon after falling out of a broken office chair, lost wages and the billable hours your firm is losing can add up in a hurry.

The gear in the office needs to be insured, as well. Equipment insurance can be valuable if the air conditioner quits in the heat of summer and forces the design team to the nearest wifi-equipped coffee bar. Of course, if those same employees steal money or equipment from the company—a sadly common occurrence—your Employee Dishonesty policy may help you recover financially. Another policy altogether covers you if the water main under your building breaks and the firm has to relocate for weeks as the problem is fixed.

The list of possible coverage is extensive, but suffice it to say that your firm will need to look past what happens if everything goes well and insure against things going wrong. As important, these policies need to be computed as expenses and added to the cost of doing business. Your billable rate for your staff may not generate a profit if you have not accounted for the expense of insuring the firm. If you have some basic policies, such as General Liability, to get started and then add employees, the increase in insurance premiums and types of policies you will need will again force you to reevaluate your rates.

# BUSINESS MODELS

A design firm can have many forms, and creative work is done all over the world in businesses that range from a single artist to a large, multinational operation. Technology and increasingly fast and inexpensive travel have expanded the way a firm can be modeled, as coworkers can be located across state or national boundaries for clients that are hundreds of miles away from anyone on staff. A firm can still work out of a single office with local clients, and many do quite well, but others have found opportunities and business partnerships never possible before the communications revolution of the past decade. Even high-end photographers, with their large files and advanced color management, have moved to a digital workflow that enables clients to be geographically disbursed. In this section, we review how design firms have traditionally operated and then look at some of the newer forms, such as virtual firms and collectives.

## Traditional/Specialty

In a traditional design firm, there are several billing rates that coincide with skills provided to a client. A specialized firm can consist of only one person that does all the design, sells new work, and handles billing and other administrative issues. More commonly, a small firm is made up of a few established designers that have different strengths, and the designers each gravitate toward what they do best (see Figure 8–8). When you ask a firm principal how he ended up remaining a creative director or why he moved into account management, the story often goes back to the earlier days of the firm and the realization by the partners that the work needed to be divided between them. As the firm grows, a more standard organization chart forms as other employees need to report to the partners, and the founders become less directly involved in the design specifics of each project. The amount of hands on work by firm principals varies greatly between firms. Some are happy to have younger, more technology savvy designers working on the latest software and will strictly manage client relationships, whereas others never really let go of their design roots and will instead stay involved in the details while account managers are hired to take care of clients.

Most design firms run out of a small office and slowly add space as their client work increases. The stereotype that most creative firms operate from very fashionable open offices renovated from old lofts or prewar warehouses is not always the case, but many firms do shy away from an overly corporate atmosphere and instead want offices to encourage collaboration between designers. Office space is another major expense of running a firm, and buying or leasing an office must be carefully weighed, often with the advice of your accountant, based on the long-term strategy, goals, and growth projections of the firm.

SPECIALTY FIRM

VIDEO

+ SALES

+ MARKETING

PRINT

+ HIRING STAFF

+ HR

+ OFFICE SPACE

WEB

+ ACCOUNTING

+ TAXES

+ TECH SUPPORT

figure | 8–8 |

A specialty firm often starts with designers of different strengths, and business tasks are then divided among them until other staff can be hired.

Although many design firms have the ability to work with clients around the country and other parts of the world, a good local core of clients is the backbone of most creative businesses. Every city has major industries, and you will often find these businesses represented in the portfolio of a design firm. A firm based in southern California might have clients in the auto industry, but more commonly you would find their work leans toward local core industries such as the entertainment business. As such, a firm acquiring a good amount of work in a certain out-of-town industry might use that strength to establish a second office.

---

### Q&A Ask the Pros:
### Choosing Projects
### Kenn Fine, Fine Design Group

*Q: What would you advise designers that are new to the field?*
A: Turn away from projects you know are not right for you, even though they may have a big price tag. In a way, you are what you eat. If you take projects you don't want to be doing, you'll find that a few years down the line that type of project is all that you are doing.

---

One of the primary challenges of a specialty firm is winning work from clients that want a more comprehensive approach to their creative work. A design firm that does only websites, for example, would be at risk of losing clients to firms with integrated marketing experience, allowing them to provide web design as part of an overall branding campaign that includes identity, print, video, and other areas. As such, a specialty firm needs to have strong relationships in the industry, especially locally, to partner with other firms on an as-needed basis. Because design has increased in complexity and specialization, small design shops are often unable to have specialists in every area. As such, strategic partnerships between firms with different strengths can help overcome objections from clients that want a single point of contact for their creative needs.

The benefit of a specialty shop is in the depth of skills that can be brought to a client engagement. For example, an advertising firm might sell a client on television spots with intense motion graphics work that can only be accomplished with the latest software and up-to-date skills. A multidisciplinary or advertising firm is unlikely to have such skills, or the desire to invest in the required hardware and software to create the work, but a specialty firm that concentrates solely on video work would find the challenge perfectly suited to their designers.

## Multidisciplinary

Because specialties can be a hard sell to clients that want to use a single vendor for creative work, many design firms have additional skill sets on staff. A multidisciplinary firm might have areas of print design—layout, illustration, type design, and image editing—as a base with newer specialties such as interactive, motion graphics, or video added to that core discipline. Along with all these visual skills, writers often work closely with account managers to create the overall voice of a marketing campaign.

Marketing is so tied to graphic communications now that many firms have these methods and practices as a base and offer design services to compliment an overall brand management practice. Other multidisciplinary firms, especially in advertising, make the larger portion of their profits from ad placement fees—a commission paid by a television network to sell their airtime, for example—and offer design to the extent that it supports this practice. The focus of this type of practice generally is speed and consistency and not necessarily on craft. There are exceptions to this, of course, but it stands to reason that if design is a core practice of a firm founded by designers, the focus will gravitate more toward doing great work and less on placement rates.

The structure of a multidisciplinary firm is similar to a specialty firm, but extra layers are often added to support larger projects and make sure communication between disciplines is in place. Project managers work between the design specialties and ensure that timelines, billable hours, costs, purchased assets, copywriting, and final production all move forward correctly for each project. Project management is a discipline in itself that works separately from design but many effective managers have a design background so there is a deeper understanding of the challenges of each project.

Account managers in a multidisciplinary firm sell new projects to clients. Because the most effective and mutually beneficial work arrangement in design is generally longer-term clients, the account manager must continually work with clients to plan short- and long-term brand strategy, as well as contingency planning. The brand strategy is often central to the business operation and an effective account manager must understand design in the broader context of the client's situation, competitors, and industry trends.

As a multidisciplinary firm grows, it is likely to move into other territories and open multiple offices. Similar to the specialty firm though, a larger firm will normally have its core clients nearby. This may not be critical to all specialties, as certain roles such as account management might handle much of the travel to clients for all but very specific project needs. The office does allow staff of differing specialties to collaborate, and allows project managers to reallocate staff based on impending deadlines or project importance.

The challenge of a multidisciplinary firm lies in keeping all the various specialties in the office busy at the same time. This can be daunting for principals and project managers, as some designers in the firm may have very deep skills in an area that is harder to sell and others may be constantly in demand. Most design firms cannot afford to hire designers that are not billing clients at peak efficiency, so there is a balancing act between hiring full time and using freelancers to supplement the staff as project needs arise. A busy firm is likely to use both full-time specialists and freelancers, and many use these temporary assignments as a working interview. Freelancers who work well with the firm and do quality work are often extended offers for full-time positions (see Figure 8–9). This is a frequent path for designers new to the field, as well, and can lead to a full-time job with a firm as their client work increases.

## Virtual

The Internet has allowed another business model to thrive in direct competition to traditional firms. A virtual firm, usually an LLC or corporation in structure, does not have a full-time physical office location. Instead, principals, designers, project managers, and account executives work remotely—across the country or spread out around the world. The benefit is a clear reduction of

## FREELANCE TO FULLTIME

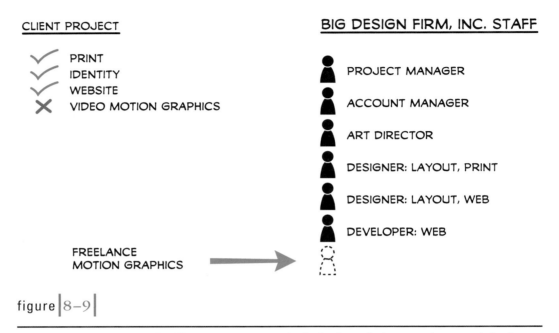

CLIENT PROJECT

✓ PRINT
✓ IDENTITY
✓ WEBSITE
✗ VIDEO MOTION GRAPHICS

FREELANCE
MOTION GRAPHICS

**BIG DESIGN FIRM, INC. STAFF**

PROJECT MANAGER

ACCOUNT MANAGER

ART DIRECTOR

DESIGNER: LAYOUT, PRINT

DESIGNER: LAYOUT, WEB

DEVELOPER: WEB

figure |8–9|

Client requirements for specific skills can create opportunity for freelance designers to showcase their talents and find full-time positions.

costs, and a distributed workforce that does not rely on a single, regional base. Without an office, a virtual firm can operate with either lower billable rates or a higher profit margin. Even factoring the costs of technology infrastructure—much of which can be rented, leased, or otherwise contracted on a per-use basis—a virtual firm can operate for far less money than a traditional office.

Because employees can work from anywhere, the firm is able to work with designers who might not otherwise want to relocate. A firm based in New York or San Francisco, for example, must contend with high cost of living when recruiting designers, especially as they get more experienced and not easily sold on the excitement of the city. The same firm, operating virtually, might use designers in many smaller, less expensive cities around the world. A virtual firm can often handle the occasional meeting that does require physical presence by video conferencing or by requiring business travel of the employees. A virtual firm might be several specialists in different locations or a team of designers in one location and account managers around the country (see Figure 8–10).

A virtual firm may use outsourcing of skilled work to developing nations, especially for web design and other technology-intensive work, but more typically design work requires deep cultural understanding that is hard to acquire remotely. However, like all skilled professionals, designers should be aware that more low-level tasks each year are sent overseas in search of more efficiency and higher profits. A designer new to the industry must face this reality by refining not only their hard skills, but also work to become a trusted advisor to clients. The working relationship

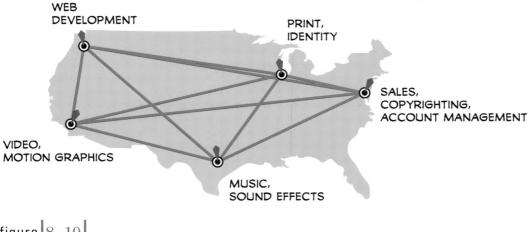

## THE VIRTUAL FIRM

WEB
DEVELOPMENT

PRINT,
IDENTITY

SALES,
COPYRIGHTING,
ACCOUNT MANAGEMENT

VIDEO,
MOTION GRAPHICS

MUSIC,
SOUND EFFECTS

figure |8–10|

The virtual firm has no single office location, but instead brings together talent by using the Internet to collaborate on projects.

with clients, along with a true understanding of their business and the challenges they face is the hardest layer to outsource, and strengthening these ties may secure your employment as designers in developing nations continue to become proficient at high-end design software.

The downside of a virtual firm is that aside from occasional in-person meetings all the back and forth collaboration of a project must frequently be done online and by phone. This requires excellent communication skills—as much or more than a traditional firm—because email will replace many quick discussions that might happen in the break room or the hallway at a firm with a physical space.

### The Occasional Office

Many established designers are uncomfortable with the virtual firm setup because they do, on occasion, need to work together in person or use a conference room to make a pitch to a prospective client. The answer is surprisingly simple (and surprisingly common)— virtual office space. With a virtual office, the firm can rent fully furnished workspace or conference rooms—some equipped with video conferencing, projectors, whiteboards, and other perks—by the hour or the day. This does not give the firm the cool urban renewal loft space in the warehouse district, but it does give them a modern, air-conditioned, professional appearance with phone and Internet connections, and allows in-person collaboration without three espresso machines frothing in the background. One of the major companies that lease virtual office space claims almost half the Fortune 500 as clients, so while the concept is relatively new to design, other professional services—including some of the big names in consulting—have used remote workforces for years.

Another concern with a virtual firm is security. Distributing files across the world means multiple points of failure and increased risk of computer viruses. A virtual firm must plan around these issues and have servers and backup systems in place so that a person leaving the firm does not take half the company portfolio or all the financial statements with them. Without these checks and balances, some clients may be hesitant to award sensitive work that requires nondisclosure agreements.

Also lost in the virtual firm is an office culture. There is no real shared experience of working on a project, so managers must be very savvy about keeping everyone aligned with the company goals and direction and not letting the virtual aspect turn into a loose network of freelance talent.

Finally, a virtual firm must make the client comfortable that the work will be the same caliber, the same efficiency, and the same (or lower) cost as that of a traditional firm. Because so many companies now make use of remote workers, the virtual firm does not have as difficult a presentation as they once did. That said, the virtual firm can very easily come across as science fiction, especially selling to established industries that want the perceived value of a traditional creative services firm with a physical location.

## Cooperative

A cooperative, also known as a consortium, is a group of designers or design firms that work together for a common purpose. This is usually done for some charitable cause, such as to help raise awareness for abused animals. A group of interested designers might take up the cause to create street posters, shirts, or other materials to spread the message of a nonprofit organization or its primary desired outcome.

Apart from the positive feelings generated by using design for a good cause, the members of the cooperative may form strong business ties and get a chance to push their creative expression in a new direction. Work donated to nonprofits can often be tax deduction, so the designers may want to consult an accountant before approaching the project as a strictly artistic pursuit. This is especially true if the designer does paid freelance work and is responsible for taxes.

A cooperative can be an effective for-profit entity as well. For example, designers from several firms who share a passion for a certain design methodology, such as standards-based web design, may agree to work in their spare time as part of a collective. In this case, the collective is doing work that may be materially similar to their employers, but the focus is on promoting and emphasizing the benefits of their chosen method. Other collectives may form around other methodologies, from graffiti art to lead typesetting, or by other common interests within the design community. In either case, if the collective is going to engage in profitable activities it would be best served to form a business—a partnership or perhaps corporation of some type—to ensure there is no legal liability from the work.

An interesting aspect of collectives is also the ability to form and disappear in a short amount of time. A collective, as something that generally comes into existence by casual agreement of designers, may only finish one project or take one client per year as a sort of working vacation for more routine assignments. Some design firms even welcome this participation as something that generates positive coverage in the design press, has a positive effect on the design community, and serves to sharpen skills and inspire creative professionals.

- In a sole proprietorship, the owner does not have to consult partners or shareholders to make decisions but is not afforded legal protection.
- The *limited partnership* (LP) allows the business to have additional owners aside from the general partners, called limited partners, who are only liable to the extent of their investment in the firm and cannot actively manage the business.
- A corporation differs from a partnership in several ways, but the most important to the prospective firm owner is that the corporation is a separate legal entity from the shareholders.
- The LLC is a legal structure that combines many of the most desirable aspects of corporations and partnerships.
- Your accountant may prepare end-of-the-year tax preparation, but will likely offer additional services for your design firm and proactively recommend how to handle various financial decisions that impact your firm and act as a strategic partner.
- A lawsuit is a manageable risk and does not affect the vast majority of designers.
- At a minimum, your attorney should review contracts, proposals, and any binding documents signed with clients, suppliers, employees, or partner firms.
- Business insurance can reimburse you for some unforeseen losses including equipment, fraud, theft, company transportation, and others.
- Most creative businesses have a group of local clients and build from this base.

**IMPORTANT! READ CAREFULLY:** This End User License Agreement ("Agreement") sets forth the conditions by which Cengage Learning will make electronic access to the Cengage Learning-owned licensed content and associated media, software, documentation, printed materials, and electronic documentation contained in this package and/or made available to you via this product (the "Licensed Content"), available to you (the "End User"). BY CLICKING THE "I ACCEPT" BUTTON AND/OR OPENING THIS PACKAGE, YOU ACKNOWLEDGE THAT YOU HAVE READ ALL OF THE TERMS AND CONDITIONS, AND THAT YOU AGREE TO BE BOUND BY ITS TERMS, CONDITIONS, AND ALL APPLICABLE LAWS AND REGULATIONS GOVERNING THE USE OF THE LICENSED CONTENT.

## 1.0 SCOPE OF LICENSE

1.1 <u>Licensed Content</u>. The Licensed Content may contain portions of modifiable content ("Modifiable Content") and content which may not be modified or otherwise altered by the End User ("Non-Modifiable Content"). For purposes of this Agreement, Modifiable Content and Non-Modifiable Content may be collectively referred to herein as the "Licensed Content." All Licensed Content shall be considered Non-Modifiable Content, unless such Licensed Content is presented to the End User in a modifiable format and it is clearly indicated that modification of the Licensed Content is permitted.

1.2 Subject to the End User's compliance with the terms and conditions of this Agreement, Cengage Learning hereby grants the End User, a nontransferable, nonexclusive, limited right to access and view a single copy of the Licensed Content on a single personal computer system for noncommercial, internal, personal use only. The End User shall not (i) reproduce, copy, modify (except in the case of Modifiable Content), distribute, display, transfer, sublicense, prepare derivative work(s) based on, sell, exchange, barter or transfer, rent, lease, loan, resell, or in any other manner exploit the Licensed Content; (ii) remove, obscure, or alter any notice of Cengage Learning's intellectual property rights present on or in the Licensed Content, including, but not limited to, copyright, trademark, and/or patent notices; or (iii) disassemble, decompile, translate, reverse engineer, or otherwise reduce the Licensed Content.

## 2.0 TERMINATION

2.1 Cengage Learning may at any time (without prejudice to its other rights or remedies) immediately terminate this Agreement and/or suspend access to some or all of the Licensed Content, in the event that the End User does not comply with any of the terms and conditions of this Agreement. In the event of such termination by Cengage Learning, the End User shall immediately return any and all copies of the Licensed Content to Cengage Learning.

## 3.0 PROPRIETARY RIGHTS

3.1 The End User acknowledges that Cengage Learning owns all rights, title and interest, including, but not limited to all copyright rights therein, in and to the Licensed Content, and that the End User shall not take any action inconsistent with such ownership. The Licensed Content is protected by U.S., Canadian and other applicable copyright laws and by international treaties, including the Berne Convention and the Universal Copyright Convention. Nothing contained in this Agreement shall be construed as granting the End User any ownership rights in or to the Licensed Content.

3.2 Cengage Learning reserves the right at any time to withdraw from the Licensed Content any item or part of an item for which it no longer retains the right to publish, or which it has reasonable grounds to believe infringes copyright or is defamatory, unlawful, or otherwise objectionable.

## 4.0 PROTECTION AND SECURITY

4.1 The End User shall use its best efforts and take all reasonable steps to safeguard its copy of the Licensed Content to ensure that no unauthorized reproduction, publication, disclosure, modification, or distribution of the Licensed Content, in whole or in part, is made. To the extent that the End User becomes aware of any such unauthorized use of the Licensed Content, the End User shall immediately notify Cengage Learning. Notification of such violations may be made by sending an e-mail to infringement@cengage.com.

## 5.0 MISUSE OF THE LICENSED PRODUCT

5.1 In the event that the End User uses the Licensed Content in violation of this Agreement, Cengage Learning shall have the option of electing liquidated damages, which shall include all profits generated by the End User's use of the Licensed Content plus interest computed at the maximum rate permitted by law and all legal fees and other expenses incurred by Cengage Learning in enforcing its rights, plus penalties.

## 6.0 FEDERAL GOVERNMENT CLIENTS

6.1 Except as expressly authorized by Cengage Learning, Federal Government clients obtain only the rights specified in this Agreement and no other rights. The Government acknowledges that (i) all software and related documentation incorporated in the Licensed Content is existing commercial computer software within the meaning of FAR 27.405(b)(2); and (2) all other data delivered in whatever form, is limited rights data within the meaning of FAR 27.401. The restrictions in this section are acceptable as consistent with the Government's need for software and other data under this Agreement.

## 7.0 DISCLAIMER OF WARRANTIES AND LIABILITIES

7.1 Although Cengage Learning believes the Licensed Content to be reliable, Cengage Learning does not guarantee or warrant (i) any information or materials contained in or produced by the Licensed Content, (ii) the accuracy, completeness or reliability of the Licensed Content, or (iii) that the Licensed Content is free from errors or other material defects. THE LICENSED PRODUCT IS PROVIDED "AS IS," WITHOUT ANY WARRANTY OF ANY KIND AND CENGAGE LEARNING DISCLAIMS ANY AND ALL WARRANTIES, EXPRESSED OR IMPLIED, INCLUDING, WITHOUT LIMITATION, WARRANTIES OF MERCHANTABILITY OR FITNESS FOR A PARTICULAR PURPOSE. IN NO EVENT SHALL CENGAGE LEARNING BE LIABLE FOR: INDIRECT, SPECIAL, PUNITIVE OR CONSEQUENTIAL DAMAGES INCLUDING FOR LOST PROFITS, LOST DATA, OR OTHERWISE. IN NO EVENT SHALL CENGAGE LEARNING'S AGGREGATE LIABILITY HEREUNDER, WHETHER ARISING IN CONTRACT, TORT, STRICT LIABILITY OR OTHERWISE, EXCEED THE AMOUNT OF FEES PAID BY THE END USER HEREUNDER FOR THE LICENSE OF THE LICENSED CONTENT.

## 8.0 GENERAL

8.1 <u>Entire Agreement</u>. This Agreement shall constitute the entire Agreement between the Parties and supercedes all prior Agreements and understandings oral or written relating to the subject matter hereof.

8.2 <u>Enhancements/Modifications of Licensed Content</u>. From time to time, and in Cengage Learning's sole discretion, Cengage Learning may advise the End User of updates, upgrades, enhancements and/or improvements to the Licensed Content, and may permit the End User to access and use, subject to the terms and conditions of this Agreement, such modifications, upon payment of prices as may be established by Cengage Learning.

8.3 <u>No Export</u>. The End User shall use the Licensed Content solely in the United States and shall not transfer or export, directly or indirectly, the Licensed Content outside the United States.

8.4 <u>Severability</u>. If any provision of this Agreement is invalid, illegal, or unenforceable under any applicable statute or rule of law, the provision shall be deemed omitted to the extent that it is invalid, illegal, or unenforceable. In such a case, the remainder of the Agreement shall be construed in a manner as to give greatest effect to the original intention of the parties hereto.

8.5 <u>Waiver</u>. The waiver of any right or failure of either party to exercise in any respect any right provided in this Agreement in any instance shall not be deemed to be a waiver of such right in the future or a waiver of any other right under this Agreement.

8.6 <u>Choice of Law/Venue</u>. This Agreement shall be interpreted, construed, and governed by and in accordance with the laws of the State of New York, applicable to contracts executed and to be wholly preformed therein, without regard to its principles governing conflicts of law. Each party agrees that any proceeding arising out of or relating to this Agreement or the breach or threatened breach of this Agreement may be commenced and prosecuted in a court in the State and County of New York. Each party consents and submits to the nonexclusive personal jurisdiction of any court in the State and County of New York in respect of any such proceeding.

8.7 <u>Acknowledgment</u>. By opening this package and/or by accessing the Licensed Content on this Web site, THE END USER ACKNOWLEDGES THAT IT HAS READ THIS AGREEMENT, UNDERSTANDS IT, AND AGREES TO BE BOUND BY ITS TERMS AND CONDITIONS. IF YOU DO NOT ACCEPT THESE TERMS AND CONDITIONS, YOU MUST NOT ACCESS THE LICENSED CONTENT AND RETURN THE LICENSED PRODUCT TO CENGAGE LEARNING (WITHIN 30 CALENDAR DAYS OF THE END USER'S PURCHASE) WITH PROOF OF PAYMENT ACCEPTABLE TO CENGAGE LEARNING, FOR A CREDIT OR A REFUND. Should the End User have any questions/comments regarding this Agreement, please contact Cengage Learning at Delmar.help@cengage.com.